S0-CFM-113
Cheryl
Wishing you
the best
3-27-96

ACCORDION MAN

ne Legendary

Dick Contino

by Bob Bove with Lou Angellotti

ACCORDION MAN

Manufactured in the United States of America

PUBLISHING, INC.
4909 N. Monroe Street
Tallahassee, Florida 32303

ISBN: 0-942407-29-6

This book is dedicated to
LEIGH SNOWDEN CONTINO —
one of the finest, gentlest and most
beautiful women who ever lived.

Special Thanks

"As I read Bob Bove's wonderful book about me, many memories, some long dormant, flooded my mind. My early years in Fresno, the support afforded me by my wonderful parents, my accordion training with Maestro Angelo Cognazzo, my entry into the world of show business under the direction of Mr. Horace Heidt, the beginning of my career as a solo artist, my troubles with the government and subsequent military experience — all these things are related in a clear, concise manner that tells 'my side of the story.' More importantly, however, the book touches on many of the people who have had such an impact in my life — my loving wife, Leigh; my beautiful children (Mary, Cathy, Deidre, Robert, and Peter); the members of my fan club who've stayed with me through good times and bad; celebrities such as Frank Sinatra and Ed Sullivan who supported my career when others turned their backs on me; good friends like Al and Linda Waltner, Leo Held and Joe Petosa; Paul Iannelli and Anthony Fornelli, the people who helped revitalize my career through the famed Italian fests at Milwaukee and Chicago; and, of course, Bob Bove himself, a man who, time and again, has shown me the true meaning of friendship and loyalty.

I sincerely hope that you've enjoyed this book and trust that it has given you a better insight into my life and career.

Dick Contino

"Finally, the true story of my son
has been written in this book."

Mary Contino

Contents

Part One

Part Two

CONTENTS

My Inspiration for Writing this Book

This book follows Contino's career from his discharge from the Army in 1954, until the present day. Peopled with a "Who's Who of Hollywood and the music industry," the book examines the highs and lows of Contino's life. From his marriage to the beautiful actress, Leigh Snowden, to his tour of Russia as part of a cultural exchange arranged by the United States Department of State and Ed Sullivan; from his performances at private parties for mobsters, to his appearances at run-down clubs with ten people in the audience; from the depths of despair when, accosted as "a no-good draft dodger," he sought solace in liquor, to the renaissance of his career at the fabulous ethnic festivals in Milwaukee and Chicago, Dick Contino's story is one that is filled with perseverance and commitment.

Inspired to write this book to set straight the story of Contino's life, the author hopes that the work fills the void that, until now, has existed concerning the entertainer's military career and subsequent life. In the face of tremendous adversity, Contino righted his life with the assistance of a loving family, a devoted friend, and his countless fans. We believe that this book will help you gain a better insight into the life of one of America's premier entertainers.

Bob Bove

Prologue

Like the homes of many young people of Italian ancestry, mine was filled with the love of music. As the youngest of eight children, I studied the accordion, an instrument of beauty and power. While practicing, I dreamed of becoming a great and famous musician, one who would have legions of fans and who would acquire riches beyond compare.

At the same time, across the country in the middle-class town of Fresno, California, another young Italian, Dick Contino, was also studying the accordion and his talent on the instrument would make him famous around the world.

In 1947 and 1948, while still in school, I, along with countless millions, followed Contino's journey to success on the Horace Heidt Talent Hunt. With each week that passed, his popularity increased. Fan clubs sprung up across the country, cards and letters poured in, and girls swooned in the aisle whenever he appeared. Overnight, Dick Contino had become one of the biggest stars in America.

As I listened to each week's program, I came to realize that Dick Contino was living my dream. I was excited by his success, although to tell the truth, I was a little envious, too. Little did I know that, in a few short years, Dick Contino, a man whose controversial jailing during the Korean war - a jail sentence that would cost him the stardom he'd worked so hard to achieve; a man who, even after serving his country, would suffer from biased and unfair publicity - would become my good friend.

Part One

CHAPTER ONE
THE YOUNG VIRTUOSO

The United States in the late 1940's was a magical and glorious place. The war to end all wars had been won — Hitler and Mussolini were dead and Hirohito was a broken man on an island in the Pacific. The Cold War lay years in the future. Things began to return to the way they'd been before the conflict.

On the West Coast a young man was beginning to gain fame for his ability with an accordion. Dick Contino was born in Fresno, California on January 17, 1930, the first of four children who would be born to Peter and Mary Contino. Contino's Sicilian-born father was a butcher who ran a small meat market in this sleepy California town. His mother, who had been born in Pittsburgh, Pennsylvania, kept house and tended the children.

"I had a happy childhood," Dick says. "Like most kids growing up during that time and in that place, I had work to do. I was learning butchering from my father. The work was hard, but it was the kind of work that made you feel good about yourself."

At Fresno High, Contino was a good, but not outstanding student. His favorite subject was art. As for athletics, Contino succumbed to a passion for football. He threw himself into the game with typical Contino ferocity and eventually became the starting fullback on the varsity squad. His stardom on the gridiron was short-lived, however. Peter Contino, upon learning that his son was "wasting his time playing games," forced him to quit the team.

"I really wanted to keep playing football," Dick recalls, "but, as in any Italian home, my father's word was law."

While Contino's father rebelled at the idea of his son's spending time on the football field, he embraced his son's passion for the accordion. Papa Contino had learned to play the accordion as a boy in Sicily and it was he who had prompted his son's interest in the instrument. As the boy progressed, his father recognized the need for professional instruction and Dick began traveling to San Francisco for lessons. For six years, Contino would spend every Friday in the studio of his teacher, Angelo Cognazzo, honing the skills that would make Dick Contino a legend. Cognazzo, a famed maestro, limited his teaching to twelve students at any one time. In recognition of Contino's awesome talent however, Cognazzo broke that self-imposed rule and accepted Contino as a student. So impressed was he with the young man that the mentor even arranged for Contino to live with him.

Those days with Cognazzo were some of the happiest of Contino's life. While the maestro was a strict instructor — a stickler for technique — he infused in each lesson a kindness and warmth that fanned the affection the young Contino has always felt for him.

"I remember one afternoon as if it were yesterday," Dick recalls with a smile. "I had finished my lesson and had gone upstairs to my room. I began to practice the lesson when, suddenly, I thought of a different way of interpreting the song I was playing."

Contino began the practice number again. This time, though,

he started to improvise, making slight changes in the rhythm and extending the bridge. Pleased with his "arrangement," Contino continued the number. After several seconds had passed, the accordionist's reverie was shattered.

"I was about to cut loose with a wild passage when Cognazzo began beating against the floor with a broom stick," Dick laughingly recalls. "The message was clear — cut the clowning and get back to work!"

After about a year, much to Contino's regret, Cognazzo told him that the time had come for him to return home. As Cognazzo noted, "I hated to see Dick leave, but there was nothing more that I could teach him."

When he returned home, Contino worked as a delivery boy in his father's market. Whenever he found a spare moment, though, he would pick up his accordion and practice at perfecting his technique.

"I know that it sounds like something out of one of those Mickey Rooney and Judy Garland movies," Dick laughs, "but, I swear, I always kept my accordion handy while working in the market and practiced whenever I could. I knew, even then, that my accordion would be my ticket to bigger and better things."

To further improve his proficiency, Contino played his accordion at school assemblies and dances. His music made him so popular that the boys, some of whom had given him a hard time for quitting the football team, once again embraced him. As for girls, well, Dick Contino never had any trouble getting attention from them.

After graduating from Fresno High in 1947, Contino enrolled at Fresno State College. Try as he might, however, he couldn't concentrate on his studies.

"I enjoyed college, but, while attending classes I kept

thinking that, if I was going to be a success, it would be my music that would take me there."

Having made that decision, Contino left college. He returned to his father's shop and devoted the majority of his time to practicing the accordion, striving for the perfection that would propel him up the ladder of success.

Dick repairing his accordion at home in Glendale, California, 1948

CHAPTER TWO

THE BIG TIME BECKONS

While waiting for his big break, Contino continued to display his virtuosity on the accordion whenever and wherever he could. Family, friends, local clubs and organizations — whenever the opportunity arose, the handsome Italian with the flashing dark eyes and magical fingers would perform.

"I remember when I'd visit friends and relatives, going from house to house playing my accordion," Dick says. "I enjoyed seeing the pleasure that my music brought to people. Many's the time that I would play 'til daybreak."

While gaining a reputation on the local level was flattering, Contino longed for something more. He had a hunger to pursue fame and fortune and he knew that playing dances and church halls around Fresno wasn't the way to achieve his dream. Then, a few weeks after leaving college, the break that Contino sought came his way.

In the early forties, Horace Heidt, a great showman and band leader, decided to go on the radio. His vehicle would be the "Original Youth Opportunity Program." Heidt's show was dedicated to offering the American public the finest in entertainment. It also would provide talented young people from across the country with the opportunity to display their talent.

Heidt believed that the best way to attract new talent was to take his program directly to the people. In that way, talented people who would not, or could not, leave the security of their home, job or family for a fling at stardom in New York or Hollywood would still have a chance at being "discovered."

This was clearly a radical concept. Shows of that era were never broadcast on location. Heidt wanted to avoid the typical ballyhooed premiere of most radio programs so he decided to schedule his first broadcast for a typical American town — Fresno, California. Alan Bode, an advance man for the show, traveled to the central California city and began to comb the area for talent; talent that might appear on the show and have a chance at the golden ring with the American people acting as judge.

The day Bode arrived in Fresno was the day that Dick Contino's life was forever changed.

Contino walked into the Musician's Union office one morning to get a transfer to do some work around Los Angeles — some friends wanted him to perform at a dance they were promoting. The secretary of the union, Henry Boetcher, called Dick over to his desk where he introduced him to a man he hadn't seen before.

That man that was Alan Bode.

"They tell me you're pretty good on the accordion," he said, eyeing Contino carefully.

"I do the best I can and the people seem to like my music."

The union man nodded to the talent scout. Bode asked Contino if he might play for him on the following day.

"If your playing's as good as I've heard, then maybe — just maybe — we might be able to use you for a show we're planning," Bode explained.

Filled with excitement, Contino offered to get his instrument and play for the man that very afternoon.

"That's okay, kid," the man smiled, "tomorrow'll be soon enough. Be here at three o'clock."

Contino walked from the union office, but his feet never touched the ground. He knew that this was his big chance — the opportunity he'd been waiting for. On his way home, he decided that he wouldn't tell his parents about the audition.

"There's no point in getting their hopes up. If they get too excited and I blow this chance, they'll be heart-broken."

Deep inside, though, Dick Contino knew that he couldn't let this opportunity pass.

CHAPTER THREE
AUDITION TIME

Early the next morning Contino took his accordion from its case and began to practice the numbers that he would perform during his audition. He had hardly slept a wink, lying in bed, thinking of all the things that had led him to this point.

"I knew that I was good enough to pass the audition," he remembers. "I wasn't being cocky — I just knew that I'd been preparing for this chance for years. Still, I couldn't help but be worried that something might go wrong."

All morning Contino readied himself for the audition. His fingers worked themselves across the keys as he worked tirelessly to perfect the songs in his rich repertoire. Early in the afternoon, after showering and dressing in his best pin-striped suit, he was about to leave for his appointment.

"Where are you going, Figlio?" his mother asked.

The boy hated to lie to his mother, but he didn't want her to be nervous about the audition.

"I'm going out for a while, Ma," he answered. "I have to see a friend."

His mother kissed him good-bye. Contino knew that the kiss would bring him all the luck that he would need.

Arriving at the Musician's Union office, Contino found the talent scout waiting for him.

"You're right on time, Dick" the man said, in a friendly voice. "That's good. The first thing an entertainer must learn is the importance of being on time for every performance."

Contino nodded his agreement and walked to the back of the office where the audition was to be held. As he adjusted his accordion, a sense of calm came over him. He began to play, softly at first, causing the talent scout to sit forward in his chair. Feeling the music, Contino began to play louder, his fingers rushing over the keys the way water rushes over a fall. Finishing with a flourish, Contino put everything he had into "Lady of Spain," the song that was to become his signature.

Though Contino had finished playing, the talent scout continued to sit for a while, just looking at the young virtuoso. Contino was growing apprehensive — surely the man wouldn't tell him that he shouldn't have come; that he wasn't good enough to be on the show! He wanted the man to speak ... to say something, anything!

Finally, Bode rose to his feet. He searched Contino's eyes.

"Horace Heidt will be in town in a few days. Give me your phone number and I'll arrange for you to play for him."

"Horace Heidt! You want me to play for Horace Heidt!"

The young man's mind raced as he thought about what music he'd play; what clothes he'd wear; how he'd carry himself.

"Now listen, Dick," the talent scout continued, "Mr. Heidt is the one who'll decide whether or not you'll appear on the program. Understand?"

Contino nodded. He wanted to ask Bode a million questions — Did you really enjoy my playing? What was Horace Heidt like? Do you really think that I'm good enough to appear on his program?

The talent scout's words broke into his thoughts.

"You didn't ask me, but I'll tell you anyway," the man said calmly. "You play for him the way that you played for me and you're a cinch to make the program. Hell, you're as good as anyone I've ever heard!"

After shaking the man's hand, Contino left the union office with a smile on his face. He had many things to do, but none was as important as what he was going to do now. He had to hurry home to tell his parents the great news!

CHAPTER FOUR
HORACE HEIDT

The next three days seemed a blur to Contino as he waited for Heidt's call. With every hour that passed Contino was afraid that something had happened and that the famous showman wasn't going to call.

"Don't worry, Figlio," his mother would whisper. "The man will call and you'll be the star of the show."

Contino smiled at his mother, remembering the excitement that had nearly overcome his parents when he told them of the audition. Mama Contino had wept with joy, pulling her eldest son to her breast and smothering him in kisses. His father, while not as demonstrative as his wife, hugged Contino. Then, looking him in the eye, he took the young man's hand and brought it to his chest.

"You will do it, my son," Contino's father said, "because you deserve to do it. For years you have practiced, learning the music and perfecting your talent. You are a great accordionist, a maestro. I never told you this until now because I thought that someone else, someone in the music business, should recognize your talent. Now, that day has come. I can say, without fear of contradiction, that my son is a master musician."

Contino looked at his father and saw the tears welling in the older man's eyes.

"I love you, Pop," Dick said, kissing his father's cheek. "No matter what happens, this will always be one of the happiest days of my life. Today, I became an artist in the eyes of the man that I respect the most."

Father and son embraced.

"I must return to the market," Papa Contino said after awhile, releasing his son from his grasp. "I can't stand around all day and act like a sentimental old man."

Contino watched his father leave. As he disappeared around the corner, Dick Contino knew that he would become a star — his father had willed it!"

•••••••••

Early the next day, the telephone rang. It was Horace Heidt's personal assistant asking Contino to come to the hotel where the impresario and his staff were staying. She explained that Heidt would meet each of the performers recommended by the talent scouts, listen to their audition and then select those who would perform on the program.

"Be here at 2:30 this afternoon," the secretary told him, "and be sure to bring along your accordion."

Unlike the morning of his previous audition, Contino was strangely calm as he prepared for the afternoon meeting. He knew now — his father had told him so — that he possessed the talent that was necessary to make it onto the program; indeed the talent to become a star. He watched the time pass with a feeling of peace unlike any he'd known before.

Dressed in a beige-wool sportcoat and brown gabardine slacks, a white shirt, a brown paisley silk tie, and brown and white two-toned shoes, Contino entered the hotel fifteen minutes before his appointment. He walked to the desk to ask the clerk where Mr. Heidt would be conducting the auditions. Contino was directed to the ballroom. As he entered, he found a scene of bustling activity. Recognizing Alan Bode, Contino walked to the man's side.

"Dick," the man said, with obvious warmth in his voice, "I'm glad you're here!"

"Hello, Mr. Bode. I want you to know that I'll try to justify your faith in me by playing my best this afternoon."

"You'll be fine," the man said smiling. As the pair talked, the talent scout told Contino about the line-up for the afternoon.

"Horace is looking forward to hearing you," he said. "You'll be the third performer on the list and, don't worry, you're gonna knock 'em dead."

Carrying his accordion, Contino walked to some chairs that had been placed in the back of the room. He set down his accordion case and settled back to watch all that was happening with a child-like interest. About fifteen minutes after he'd arrived, a tall, elegant man wearing a tailored charcoal-gray double-breasted suit entered the room. Contino saw several people hurry over to shake the man's hand and he knew that this had to be Horace Heidt.

After conversing with several people, including the agent who'd auditioned Contino, Heidt walked to where the young man was seated.

"Hello," he said, extending his hand in greeting, "I'm Horace Heidt."

Contino jumped to his feet and took the man's hand.

"Mr. H-Heidt ...," Contino stammered. "I'm very pleased to meet you."

Recognizing the young man's anxiety, Heidt placed his arm around Contino's shoulder and drew him close.

"Relax, Dick," the man said quietly, "I've heard all about you and I can't wait to hear you play."

Contino was stunned! Horace Heidt had heard of him! He couldn't wait to hear him play!

The few words from the band leader had a remarkable effect on the boy. The brief conversation had provided Dick with a sense of calm that pervaded his entire being. With a serene smile on his face, he returned to his seat to await his opportunity.

"Dick Contino .... Dick Contino .... DICK CONTINO!"

At the sound of his name, Contino awakened from his reverie. He jumped to his feet.

"Here," Contino called. He picked up his case and advanced toward the stage. As he started up the steps, Heidt gave him a grin and placed his thumb and forefinger together in a sign of approval.

"Hello, Mr. Heidt," the young man said as he hoisted the accordion onto his shoulders. "My name's Dick Contino and I'd like to play some songs for you."

For the next ten minutes, Contino played a series of tunes that held the assembled throng in a state of rapt attention. Everyone — Heidt, the talent scouts, the other contestants, and even the workers setting up the room — listened intently. When Contino had finished, Heidt jumped to his feet.

"Great, Dick," the impresario clapped, "just great! Be at the theater at 6:00 on the night of the 7th. You're gonna be on the radio, Son!"

CHAPTER FIVE
VICTORY IS HIS

The night of December 7, 1947, was calm, cool and clear. An overflow throng of nearly six hundred people jammed the theater where the Horace Heidt - Philip Morris program would be broadcast across the whole United States.

As instructed, Contino arrived at the theater precisely at six p.m. Accompanying him that evening were his parents, brothers, sister, aunts, uncles, cousins, and dozens of friends.

"The excitement was overwhelming," Contino remembers. "People were saying that the show was the biggest thing that had ever happened to Fresno and I could hardly believe that I was going to be a part of it.

As his parents turned to enter the theater, Contino took them into his arms. Before ending the embrace, the boy whispered to them, "Tonight I'll make you proud."

Then, with a wave and a smile, Dick Contino headed for the stage.

•••••••••

Getting ready for his performance, Contino was prepared to use song arrangements made famous by three of his idols — Ernie Felice, Art Van Damme and Charlie Magnante.

As he ran through a portion of each arrangement, Heidt listened intently. Finally, he stepped to Contino's side.

"I don't think that any of those arrangements will be too effective, Dick," he said, deep in thought. "Why don't you play that tune where you shake the accordion?"

Shaking the bellows was something that Contino had improvised to break-up the monotony of practice. To his surprise, however, people loved the technique and it never failed to create excitement amongst his audience.

"You mean 'Lady of Spain'?" he asked Heidt.

The maestro nodded.

••••••••••

Horace Heidt, resplendent in a black silk dinner jacket, raised his hands to quiet the crowd.

"Ladies and Gentlemen! Boys and Girls!" the showman announced. "I think you'll all agree that we've seen some marvelous entertainment tonight."

The crowd roared its enthusiastic response. "And now, for the final performer for the evening ... here's Dick Contino!"

Contino ducked through the stage curtain. He appeared to a thunderous ovation. As he adjusted his accordion, the young man worked the crowd, flashing his brightest smile and winking to the bobbysoxers who had crammed into the front rows of the theater. After a slight pause, Contino launched into a volcanic rendition of "Lady of Spain." From the very first notes, the audience began to clap in time to the rhythm of the song. Sensing that he held the audience in the palm of his hand, Contino increased the tempo, his fingers dashing across the keys. Bobbing his head in time to the music, he again beamed that dazzling smile and the audience burst into frenzied applause. Nodding towards Heidt, Contino began to shake the bellows on his accordion, enhancing the classic tune with a new and distinctive sound. The young girls screamed his name over and over again. As Contino poured everything he had into the closing notes of the song, the audience responded in kind. Finishing with a flourish, the beads of sweat stood against his forehead, while the wave of applause that cascaded across the stage began to send the needle on the applause meter higher and higher. After a few seconds, the needle had passed the previous marks achieved by the evening's performers. Victory was his! Still the audience continued its ovation, stomping, clapping, whistling, cheering. Even the appearance of Horace Heidt raising his hands for silence, failed to dim the enthusiasm of the crowd. It was two full minutes after the song had ended before the furor subsided. Basking in the glow of the adulation that he'd worked so hard to achieve, Dick stood smiling next to Heidt as the bandmaster took his hand.

"Ladies and gentleman," Heidt called, time and again to overcome the cheers of the crowd, "we have a winner. By a full thirty points on the electric applause meter, the winner of tonight's contest and the recipient of two hundred and fifty dollars is DICK CONTINO."

The cheers began again. Frantically, Contino searched the theater for his parents. Oblivious to the applause and the calling of his name, the young man continued to scan the crowd until, finally, his eyes fell upon his family. Bringing his hand to his mouth, Contino launched a kiss in the direction of his parents and then mouthed the words, "I love you." The girls in the audience imagined that the kiss had been sent their way. Contino laughed at the response.

"Let them think what they like," he reasoned. "This night belongs to the people that I love most in all the world — this night belongs to my parents."

Contino smiled again, waved a good-bye, and departed the stage. In the grand tradition that is as old as time, a star had been born.

CHAPTER SIX
ON THE ROAD

Backstage, an appreciative Horace Heidt said as he stood next to Contino after the contest, "That certainly was a remarkable performance."

The young boy expressed his thanks and offered words of praise for the other performers who had appeared that evening.

"I got lucky, Mr. Heidt, the crowd just liked my song, but there were some awfully fine entertainers on the stage tonight ..."

Heidt stopped Contino with a wave of his hand.

"Dick," he said urgently, "you're right, there were some fine performers on stage tonight. There was, however, only one performer who was able to reach into the audience and lift those people right up out of their seats. And that was you, Son."

Contino didn't know what to say. Again, he thanked Heidt and mentioned that, if at all possible, he looked forward to seeing him again.

"Wait, Dick," the man said, "don't you know what happens now?"

The young man shook his head.

"Why, as tonight's winner you'll appear on next week's show in Los Angeles."

"Los Angeles? I'll be playing in Los Angeles?"

The words echoed in his ears.

"And that's not all. As long as you continue to win you'll be invited back to defend your title every week. Why, with the way you played this evening, you might wind up going all the way to New York to compete for the Quarter Final championship and a prize of seven hundred and fifty dollars."

Contino was stunned! Los Angeles, maybe even New York. A chance at the $750 prize! The chance to play in cities across the country.

"Dick, you can appear in LA next week, can't you?"

"Oh, yes, Sir. I'll be there. I'll be there with bells on!"

Leaving the theatre, Contino ran into his mother's arms, smothering her with kisses and hugs. "Figlio, you were wonderful!" she beamed.

"Mama, next week I play in Los Angeles! Isn't that great?"

The woman brought her hand to her mouth. "Dick! Los Angeles?"

She turned to her husband. "Did you hear, Papa? Dick plays in Los Angeles next week."

"That's right, Pop. And Mr. Heidt has contests planned for cities all across the country. As long as I win, I'll be invited back to appear on every show."

Tears welled in his father's eyes. Unable to speak, he nodded his assent and took his son's hand into his own.

"Papa," the boy asked, "will you and mama go with me to Los Angeles?"

"My son," his father answered softly, "we will go with you wherever you play."

••••••••••

The first stop for the young sensation was Los Angeles where the Heidt program broadcast for several successive weeks in December. Contino's fame preceded him as girls lined up hours before show time to be sure of getting seats close to the stage. Each show became a replica of the one that had preceded it. Appearing at the end of the program, Contino would come onto the stage amidst the cheers, squeals and swoons of the bobby-soxer throng and play a stirring rendition of one of the songs he would soon make famous. As he played he would flash that dazzling smile, move his body to the beat of the music and finish with a flourish. At every show the result was the same — the cheers of the fans sent the applause meter through the roof.

The ensuing weeks rushed by as Contino, accompanied by Mama and Papa Contino, traveled throughout the country, taking on all comers at contests in cities from Los Angeles to Pittsburgh.

The Los Angeles stay was beneficial in many ways for the young prodigy. In addition to winning the first-prize money for the Heidt program, Contino was introduced to prominent people in the entertainment industry.

"I had the opportunity to meet people that I'd read about most of my life," Dick says. "People like Jack Benny, Bing Crosby and Bob Hope stopped by the theater to say hello."

The weeks following the advent of 1948 saw Contino participating in contests in Omaha, Des Moines, Youngstown, Cleveland, Pittsburgh, and Harrisburg. He was victorious in each outing. Among the hopefuls he defeated was a thin, young Nebraska magician named Johnny Carson.

"I've had people ask if traveling to different cities and performing week after week was a tremendous strain," Contino says. "But, in all honesty, what could have been better? I was so excited by everything that was happening, traveling with my parents and winning the contests, that I thoroughly enjoyed myself. And, of course, I was just eighteen years old."

By the time the contest entered its tenth week, the caravan had moved on to New York. Because of the excitement the program had generated, four contests would be held, one each in the Bronx, Brooklyn, Queens, and Manhattan. Three times, in the "B-B-Q" boroughs of New York, Contino mounted the stage to overwhelming applause and walked off with the victory.

"To win in New York was an unbelievable thrill," Dick recalls. "Here I was, not a year out of high school, and I'd crossed the country doing something that I loved and getting paid for it."

"I have to admit, too, that competing for the Quarter Final championship in New York City was pretty exciting!"

The Quarter Final championship was held on February 24, 1948. This would be the greatest test of Contino's ability as he would be competing against other top performers who had been victorious in regional competitions.

The contest was broadcast from the studios of WNBC, a Manhattan radio station. Contino, once again the last performer on the program, arrived at the station a full hour before air time. Trying to control his excitement, the young man began to practice the tune that he hoped would propel him to victory.

"Hello, Dick," a familiar voice said. Contino looked up to see Horace Heidt standing before him. "How are you tonight?"

"Hi, Mr. Heidt. I'm fine, I guess. A little nervous though."

The showman put an arm around Contino's shoulders.

"Dick, relax," the maestro said, "you'll do just fine."

"I don't know ..."

"Listen," the older man said, "I've watched you for thirteen weeks now, and you're as good as any of the people you'll be performing with tonight."

"Thanks, Mr. Heidt," the youngster answered. "It's just that ..."

"Dick, trust me. I've been around for a long, long time and you're as fine an entertainer as I've seen. You have to believe in what I'm saying and, more importantly, you have to believe in yourself."

Contino looked directly into the man's eyes and smiled. "I'll be fine, Mr. Heidt," the young man said.

Heidt nodded and walked away. Contino had a look of admiration in his eyes.

"I won't let you down."

•••••••••

From a corner of the studio, Contino observed the contest unfolding. He watched intently as each entertainer walked to the microphone and performed his specialty. The one common thread that Contino noticed was that each of the youngsters seemed somewhat "stiff," perhaps affected by a case of nerves as they pondered the importance of the contest.

"I'm not going to walk on that stage like some frightened dog," Contino promised. "These people are frozen with fear. Not me. I'm gonna go out there and have some fun. Heck, if I don't enjoy myself when I play then how I can I expect anyone else to enjoy my performance?"

That realization seemed to crystallize the essence of the evening. Contino knew that people came to a show to be entertained, to feel a sense of joy and wonder at outstanding talent. Contino had experienced great success and, while much of it could be attributed to his virtuosity on the accordion, a great deal of that praise had come from the fact that he was an "entertainer," someone who enjoyed entertaining and loved putting on a winning performance. Tonight he would continue in the grand tradition of a Dick Contino performance.

Contino took the stage as the evening's fifth and final contestant. Already appreciated by the fans of New York City, loud cheers greeted his introduction.

Walking to the microphone, Contino stood for a moment, waiting for exactly the right moment to begin his song. For a few seconds, seconds that seemed an eternity, he stood with his head lowered, his fingers resting lightly on the keyboard.

"Don't hurry, don't hurry," he reminded himself. "Let it come."

Then, all at once, the handsome head was raised. The flashing eyes sparkled and a million-watt smile lit up the entire room.

The audience began to move in unison as Contino launched into the opening notes of "Flight of the Bumble Bee." By the time Contino had worked through to the reprise, many fans were on their feet. Moving in time to the beat, the fans were unashamed to show how much they enjoyed the music — to show what a good time they were having.

The cheers grew louder and louder. Each time Contino swayed to the music, the bobby-soxers would unleash a chorus of screams that caused older members of the crowd to cover their ears. At the finish, the entire audience rose as one and the applause meter registered the highest mark of the evening.

Bouncing onto the stage, Horace Heidt intoned, "Ladies and gentlemen, tonight you've had the pleasure of watching five entertainers — champions all — who have proven, beyond doubt, that the future of the entertainment world is in fine hands, indeed."

"And, now, it gives me great pleasure to announce the winner of tonight's contest and its seven hundred and fifty dollar prize. Ladies and gentlemen, I give to you a young man who will, for the next eight months, entertain with the Horace Heidt Orchestra as a guest star in cities and towns across the United States—a young man who, in December of this year, will travel to Washington, D.C. to compete in our contest's Grand Finals. Here he is .... DICK CONTINO!!!"

The excitement and enthusiasm greeting his name was unlike anything that Contino had ever experienced. Raising his arms like a triumphant prize-fighter, the young man basked in the adulation of his fans. He tried to say words of thanks, but the effort was futile. Finally, with a grin and a wave of his hand, Contino left the stage.

"Congratulations, Dick," Heidt said, "you've a big year ahead of you, Son. You are going to tour as a guest star with my orchestra. You're going to make a great deal of money, and you are going to become very, very famous."

The youngster nodded at his mentor.

"I'm looking forward to it. The chance to go on tour with you and the orchestra. The things I'll be able to do for my parents with the money I'll earn ... I don't know what to say, Sir."

"Dick, why don't you call me Horace?"

"Sure, Mr. Heidt."

Both men began to laugh — a laugh that lasted for quite some time.

CHAPTER SEVEN
THE CHAMPIONSHIP BELT

Two weeks after winning the quarter-finals in New York City, Contino began touring with Horace Heidt's Orchestra. From coast to coast, crowds flocked to theaters and ball rooms to relive the past with the familiar melodies of the Heidt orchestra and to witness the future of the entertainment world unfold in Dick Contino.

Contino would appear with the orchestra three or four times each week. He also gained additional exposure by appearing on Heidt's radio program which was broadcast each Sunday evening.

The time spent on the road with his mentor served as an educational experience for the young Contino in many different ways. Traveling with professional musicians allowed Contino the opportunity of observing how to adapt to life on the road — how to handle the travel, the hotels, and the fans.

"I was like everyone's little brother," Dick says. "The guys were great to me."

Heidt noted the growth of the young performer as the days on the road became weeks and the weeks turned into months. He took the time to teach Contino the nuances of the performing art, the ways to "work" an audience. Contino absorbed each of the elements — the brief hesitation during a song; the way of altering the presentation of a number; the methods of involving the audience as part of the performance — with his customary zeal. Heidt was pleased as he watched his protégé perfect the ways of commanding a crowd.

In cities and small towns across the country, people rushed to theaters to see Heidt and the accordion-playing phenomenon. Incorporating into his act many of the ideas culled from his conversations with Heidt, Contino became a more polished performer. Subtle changes in his musical repertoire brought new excitement to songs that Contino had been playing for years.

Before he knew it, the months had slipped by and it was time for Contino to travel to Washington D.C. for the National Grand Finals of the Horace Heidt Talent Hunt. On December 10, 1948, the youngster arrived in the nation's capitol to prepare for the contest.

"I felt very comfortable about appearing in the finals," Dick remembers. "I believed that the time that I'd spent touring with the Heidt Orchestra had prepared me far more than I could have prepared myself for the event."

The finals were held in Uline Arena on the evening of December 12, 1948. A crowd of more than 10,000 fans, young and old, black and white, men and women, boys and girls filed into the auditorium to be a part of the championship evening. Philip Morris Cigarettes would sponsor the broadcast of the contest, and the tobacco giant's president, Alfred Eline, would present the awards to the contestants.

The contest was broadcast over NBC Radio. Clem McCarthy, the famous sportscaster, was the announcer. An estimated 20,000,000 people listened to the broadcast.

Four contestants were to compete that evening. Each of these contestants had already won a quarter-final championship. Once again, Contino would close the program.

At eight o'clock that night, Horace Heidt strolled to center stage to welcome the throng to "the greatest evening of entertainment in the history of the United States."

Before beginning the contest, Heidt introduced the two gentlemen who would serve as judges for the contest: Jesse M. Donaldson, Postmaster General of the United States, and Charles F. Brannon, United States Secretary of Agriculture.

The first contestant was a teenager from Zanesville, Ohio, a young black man named Stanley Morse. Following his performance, a polite round of applause escorted the young trombonist from the stage.

Johnny Mungal, a tenor from Flint, Michigan, was the evening's second performer. The young man sang a beautiful rendition of Joyce Kilmer's "Trees," and, as he stepped away from the microphone, applause showered the stage.

The evening's third contestant was Pierce Knox, a youngster who attended the Iowa School for the Blind. Knox played the xylophone. Because of the boy's physical handicap as well as his fine ability as a musician, many felt that he would prove to be Contino's stiffest competition. As Knox played "Flight of the Bumble Bee," the audience began to stir — an obvious sign of sincere approval for the young man's performance. As the song ended, a wave of applause cascaded throughout the arena .

"When Pierce finished, I really thought that he'd won the contest," Dick recalls. "He was a wonderful musician and a fine, fine young gentleman."

Contino took the stage as the evening's final performer. The crowd, aware of his reputation as an entertainer, edged forward in their seats as the handsome young man stepped to the microphone. Using all of the techniques that he'd learned by playing with the Heidt Orchestra, the youngster began a spirited rendition of "Lover." Playing to the crowd, Contino flashed his smile, shook his head and swayed his hips. With

Dick receiving First Place Award from Horace Heidt for winning the Horace Heidt Opportunity Youth Contest in Washington, D.C.

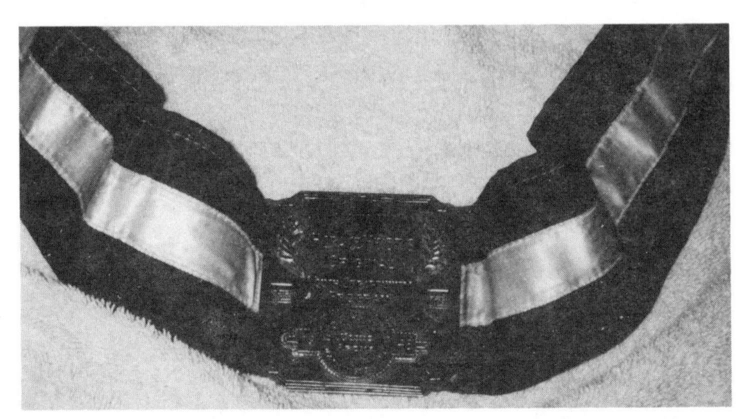

The Championship Belt Dick received after winning the Horace Heidt Youth Opportunity Contest , 1948

every move, the girls in the crowd swooned. At the number's close, many in the audience leapt to their feet and cheered, giving Contino the evening's loudest ovation.

As if in a dream, Contino stood on stage watching Horace Heidt, Alfred Eline, President of Philip Morris, and Vice-President Elect Alvin Barkley walk toward him. As each man shook his hand, the youngster began to comprehend what was happening. While the Vice-President Elect presented Heidt with an award of appreciation for his promotion of the contest, Dick accepted the congratulations of the people crowding around him.

"I've won," Contino muttered to himself, "I've won the Grand Finals!"

After what seemed an eternity, Eline stepped up to the microphone.

"Ladies and gentlemen, it is my great honor to present the Grand Prize of five thousand dollars and the gold championship belt to the winner of this evening's contest .... DICK CONTINO!!"

The ovation greeting the announcement startled Contino. So many thoughts raced through his mind that he was unsure of what to say. Mumbling his thanks, the young man waved to the audience and left the stage.

"Dick," Horace Heidt called, "congratulations! Believe me, my young friend, this is just the beginning of a wonderful career."

Contino smiled at the venerable showman. It seemed as if it was just yesterday when Contino, an unpolished young man from a small California city had begun his travels towards celebrity, fame and fortune.

What, the boy wondered, would the future hold?

Part Two

CHAPTER EIGHT
BOBBYSOXER IDOL

The days following Contino's victory in the National Finals were abuzz with activity. The young man learned that he would be placed at the head of an orchestra — an orchestra hand-picked by Horace Heidt — to headline in clubs and theaters all across the country. Hours turned into days and days into weeks as the musicians rehearsed again and again for the tour that was to be, for many, the "big break."

All the while that Contino and the orchestra worked on perfecting their rhythms, Horace Heidt offered his encouragement and, whenever requested, his advice on songs, arrangements and life on the road.

"Mr. Heidt was fabulous," Dick remembers. "With my parents having returned to Fresno, he took me under his wing and treated me like a son. I'll never forget the kindness that he showed me."

Contino, working closely with Heidt, began taking "standards," songs that were recognizable to almost every music fan, and modifying arrangements of the songs to showcase the talent of the young musician. Years later, performers like Sam Cooke, Ray Charles, Otis Redding, Joe Cocker, and Rod Stewart would carve out niches in the musical pantheon by modifying classics in such a manner but, until Contino established the precedent, altering a classic tune was considered unthinkable.

"Mr. Heidt and I spent hours at the keyboard working out charts for tunes such as "Canadian Capers" and "Torna a Sorriento." We knew that re-working the songs of great composers wouldn't be popular with everyone, but, we felt that, by creating a distinctive style of performing, I would establish an audience of my own."

After several weeks of rehearsal, Contino and his orchestra performed its first professional engagement at the Hampstead Gardens in Hampstead, New York. A throng of young fans, dating back to Contino's performances during the Heidt contest, crowded the room.

"I was afraid that our first performance would have several rough spots," Dick recalls, "but, whether it was due to the intense rehearsal or because of the warmth of the fans, the evening went off without a hitch."

Reviews for the orchestra's Hampstead performance raved about Contino's virtuosity and the artistry of his showmanship. Offers poured in. Open dates on the orchestra's schedule were filled overnight.

After several more engagements along the East Coast, Dick Contino Fan Clubs began to appear. Fueled by appearances on Heidt's radio show, by the recordings that he had made for Magnolia Records, and by his appearance on a regional broadcast of The Ed Sullivan Show, fan clubs had sprung up across the country. Wherever Contino appeared lines formed at the box office. The lines were filled with young girls — "bobbysoxers" — who turned out in numbers unparalleled since the heyday of a skinny young crooner named Frank Sinatra.

In the ensuing months, Contino would travel from coast to coast appearing with the Heidt Orchestra. Perhaps the highlight of Contino's association with the great maestro came when the orchestra appeared at the Hollywood Bowl. When Contino bounded onto the stage, he was awestricken at the sea of humanity that was awaiting his appearance. Even though he had become accustomed to the cheers and exhortations of his "bobby soxer" fans, Contino was truly amazed at the reception afforded by the 20,000 plus fans who had packed the stadium.

The tour moved from Los Angeles to San Francisco. Calling Angelo Cognazzo at his home in the bay city, Contino invited the maestro to be his guest at the show. Cognazzo gratefully accepted the invitation.

The night of the concert arrived and the arena was filled with 14,000 cheering fans. In the front row, in seats reserved for him by a grateful Contino, sat the aged Cognazzo. As the concert unfolded, Contino, although nervous at performing for the first time in front of the man who had schooled him in the intricacies of the accordion, warmed to his task. As he poured his soul into every number, he was delighted to see a look of contented satisfaction appear on his teacher's face. When the concert ended and the fans leapt to their feet to applaud Contino, Cognazzo remained in his seat. Hurrying from the stage, Contino raced to the elderly man's side.

"Dick," Cognazzo said, tears streaming down his cheeks, "you were wonderful. It is you, my son, who has now become the maestro."

The men embraced warmly and the crowd cheered the affectionate display.

••••••••••

As the months passed, Contino's growing popularity convinced him to leave the umbrella of Heidt's organization and to try his luck on his own. He was to experience his first lesson in the business of show business.

When Contino told Heidt of his plans and dreams, to Contino's great surprise, he learned that he was tied to an exclusive seven-year contract with the impresario.

To gain the freedom to pursue his artistic dreams, Contino would have to sue Heidt to void the contract. Although he respected Heidt and was grateful for what the maestro had done for him, Contino, after carefully considering the situation, went ahead with the legal action.

"It seemed that I had to break away, and he was trying to hold me back," Dick remembers. "What followed were allegations and counter-allegations — some unpleasant words were tossed about and, unfortunately, some name-calling was involved."

After a year that seemed to last an eternity, the suit was settled by representatives of the musician's union. It was agreed that Contino would stay on as a member of Heidt's organization for one more year. After that year, he would be free to leave.

"I never wanted to hurt Contino or to stifle his artistic ability," Heidt would say later while discussing the break-up.

Heidt compared his relationship with Contino to a similar arrangement that had been established between Lawrence Welk and the Lennon Sisters."

"The only difference was that the Lennon's suffered a loss of popularity when they separated from the Welk Orchestra and Contino's popularity continued to grow."

As Heidt suggested, Contino's fame and popularity "continued to grow" indeed. A news account from a 1950 Edition of the Los Angeles Times announced: "Recently, Contino left the Heidt organization to form his own troupe.

Dick and two members of his Chicago Fan Club at the Palmer House in Chicago, Il, October, 1950

Since that time, his revue has established attendance records in Kansas City, Chicago, Pittsburgh and Milwaukee."

"Those were wonderful times in spite of the controversy," Contino recalls. "One of my most cherished memories is of an afternoon in Milwaukee when fans were lined three-abreast around the city block to purchase tickets for my performance at the beautiful Riverside Theatre."

"When I arrived for rehearsal," Dick continues, "I couldn't believe what I was seeing. The fervor of the fans was unlike anything I'd ever experienced."

Later, Contino would learn even more of the fan fervor that he generated when a bobbysoxer fan, unbeknownst to her family or friends, followed him to Detroit in order to try to win the affection of the heart-throb.

"Occasionally," Dick remembers, "I would invite some fans to come backstage after the show and join me and the guys for sodas and snacks. That was how I discovered, while performing in Detroit, that the young lady had followed me from Milwaukee. I made sure that she called her parents to let her know what had happened and, then, I arranged for her to return home."

Contino's career continued to soar. In mid-1950 his soaring popularity was evidenced by the more than five hundred Dick Contino Fan Clubs that had sprung up across the country. A brilliant future lay before him.

On the horizon, however, trouble loomed. Halfway around the world in a small country called Korea — a country unknown to most Americans — the Cold War that had been simmering for five years was about to escalate into a violent confrontation.

Early in 1950, Contino began to worry about the possibility of his being drafted into the armed forces and the effect it would have on his career. Later that year, he was summoned for his draft physical. Almost immediately, he sought ways to avoid induction.

"I claimed my parents as dependents," he remembers, "and mentioned the possibility of requiring surgery on a spinal cyst. I tried every option that I thought would help keep me out of the Army."

What really affected the young star would later become

known as a neurotic condition — a phobia.

"I was experiencing this anguish, this fear of being gone, a fear of being away from my family for any length of time," Dick said. "I didn't know how to explain these feelings to people. Heck, *I* didn't understand these attacks of anxiety. So, mostly, I kept it to myself."

While Contino was experiencing these emotional difficulties, the authorities had little sympathy for someone whom they believed was searching for "an easy way out" — a superstar making a great deal of money and trying to beat the system.

In spite of his protests, Contino was judged fit for duty and assigned to Fort Ord, California, where he was to be inducted into the Army on April 13, 1951.

"The night before the induction, I suffered an anxiety attack and felt that I had to leave. My parents were in the visiting barracks and they were crying — I told the officers that I *had* to leave."

"I went to see the commanding officer and told him that I couldn't go into the service," recalls Dick. "I know that people say that I was worried about my career but, as God is my witness, I didn't care about my career at all. I even told the officer that if he could help me I'd sign a piece of paper promising that I wouldn't touch my accordion for five years. The officer was unmoved.

"Listen young man," he replied, "you're already in the army so let's cut the bull——."

Contino saw no alternative.

"I knew what I had to do," he shrugs. "I took off!"

Dick's flight from the military provided the media with front page news that lasted for months. Headlines screamed the news of Contino's disappearance and the FBI became involved in the case. After a time, Contino surrendered to federal authorities. He was indicted and went to trial.

Contino's trial was held in San Francisco. On the day he was to be sentenced, Contino stepped into an elevator and, to his surprise, encountered Judge A. P. Roche who was presiding at the trial. In the solitude of the elevator car, Contino poured out his heart to the judge, telling him that he'd changed his mind — that he would gladly serve his country. To Contino's surprise, Roche refused his offer.

"I'm not interested in your offer, Mr. Contino," the judge stated. "I've decided to use you as an example to others who seek to avoid military service."

Later that day, August 8, 1951, Dick Contino was sentenced to six months in jail and fined ten thousand dollars.

••••••••••

Contino served his sentence at McNeil Island, off the state of Washington. He served four and one-half months of his sentence before being released. In prison, he put on shows for his fellow inmates.

While in prison, Contino would receive letters from his fans throughout the country. Nearly every day, a letter would arrive from Hollywood, California. The letter was written by a beautiful talented actress whom Contino had met at one of his shows — Piper Laurie.

"Piper and I met at one of my performances," Dick recalls. "We had lots of fun together and our friendship developed into something more. We dated for a while and, soon, she began to talk of marriage."

"I loved Piper," Dick says, "but the love that I felt for her was a platonic love — the kind of love that I felt for a great friend or a sister."

The friendship that blossomed between Contino and the lovely actress endures to this day. Piper would go on to Hollywood stardom with her performance in "The Hustler," with the legendary Paul Newman, and her Academy Award nominated performance as Sissy Spacek's mother in "Carrie."

In prison, Contino became close friends with Jim Coletti, his cellmate and a convicted murderer.

"Jim Coletti was one of the nicest men I've ever met," Dick recalls fondly. "He befriended me at a time when many people turned their backs on me."

"Often, when I would get the blues, Jim gave me the support that I needed to carry on. He encouraged me to continue performing while in prison and, he never missed a performance."

"No matter what happens, I'll never forget him."

After serving his sentence, Contino was released in January of 1952. Still subject to induction into the military, he was drafted that spring. Uncle Sam had him at last.

CHAPTER NINE
THE KOREAN CONFLICT

Korea had witnessed a long history of conflict. Following the Russian - Japanese War of 1904 and 1905, the land had come under Japanese control — a control that would last until that country's surrender at the close of World War II.

After the war, Korea was divided into two sections; North and South. The North, governed by a Communist regime, became a satellite of the Soviet Union. The South, left to its own destiny, instituted democratic rule.

The Korean Conflict had exploded onto the world stage on June 25, 1950. North Korean Communist troops attacked South Korea, hoping to unify the country by force and the land once known as "Chosan" — The Land of the Morning Calm — burst into violence.

To combat the Communist invasion, forces of the United Nations, under the command of General Douglas MacArthur, rushed to the aid of South Korea. Forces from around the globe — from Australia, Canada, Greece, France, Ethiopia, Turkey, Belgium, Luxembourg, and Scotland — sent military aid to the beleaguered nation.

The conflict was referred to as a "police action." General MacArthur had even promised the American forces they'd be home by Christmas. Instead, as a result of the North Korean troops being driven back to the Yalu River — the boundary separating China and Korea — China entered the war. MacArthur, determined to destroy the Chinese supply stations, encountered

Dick taking a break during his performance in Korea; 1953

resistance from President Harry S. Truman. Truman believed the bombings would precipitate World War III. When MacArthur persisted in his efforts, the President relieved him of command.

The conflagration dragged on and on. The Korean Conflict would become one of the bloodiest wars in history. In the space of thirty-seven months of combat, more than one million Koreans were killed and millions more were forced to flee their homes. The combined casualties of the United Nations and South Korean forces totaled more than one and one-half million. The North Koreans and their Communist allies suffered casualties totaling two million killed, wounded, or missing in action.

Contino had entered the service saddled with a unique restriction — he would not be allowed to play the accordion while on active duty. He was to receive his basic training at Fort Ord, California as an infantry rifleman - a #1745 Military Order of Service.

"I knew that my orders were simply an extension of my punishment," Dick recalls, "I was to go to a front line unit as soon as I reached Korea."

Shortly before completing his basic training, Contino was approached by an officer who asked him to perform for an officer's party.

Contino explained that he couldn't perform because of his orders, but he told the officer of how I wished that he could be allowed to play for the party since it would cheer the men.

To Contino's surprise, the officer arranged for him to appear at the function.

A few days later, Contino shipped out to Seoul, the capitol of South Korea. After being assigned to the Ninth Corps, Contino met Victor Tiberi, an accordionist from Chicago

Heights, Illinois — a south suburb of the midwestern metropolis. Vic was part of a troupe headlined by singer Eddie Fisher, later to become famous for such classics as "Oh Mein Papa" and, of course, for his turbulent marriages to Debbie Reynolds, Elizabeth Taylor and Connie Stevens.

Tiberi and Fisher, learning of Contino's imminent shipment to the front line, hurriedly arranged for him to head a Special Service Entertainment Unit that would perform for troops all across Korea.

"I'll be forever grateful to Vic and Eddie for the break they gave me while I was in Korea," Dick says. "In addition to the efforts of these two fine gentlemen, I've always believed that the officer who'd arranged for me to play at the party at Fort Ord had something to do with my orders being changed so that I could enter the Special Service."

••••••••••

At the start of my senior year at the University of Dubuque, I was given a student deferment so that I might complete my college education. After graduating in June of 1951, I was called to serve my country on January 15, 1952.

Having completed my basic training at Camp Chaffee, Arkansas, I was transferred to the 44th National Guard Division of Illinois stationed at Camp Cook, California, now known as Vandenberg Air Force Base. The 44th's orders were to ship out to Korea to replace another National Guard unit that had been decimated in fierce combat with Communist forces. Since many of the casualties from the unit that we were to relieve had been from the same small town, the Army decided to send our unit to Korea as individual replacements instead of as a unit.

THE KOREAN CONFLICT

My turn came in January of 1953. After sixteen storm-tossed days on the Pacific Ocean aboard the U.S.S. General Weigel, the ship docked at Yokohama, Japan. From there, the unit was transported to the island of Hokkaido, Japan where I was assigned to the Fire Direction Center for Baker Battery, 61st Field Artillery Battalion of the First Cavalry Division.

On February 10, 1953, our battalion was shipped to Korea as a replacement artillery battalion. Arriving on February 15th, we encountered conditions that seemed unbearable. For almost three months, we endured that most terrible of sensations — not knowing if every sunset would be the last we'd ever see.

Following General Van Fleet's evacuation of the Pusan Perimeter, 40,000 unorganized North Korean troops were poised to strike at vital targets in the south. Our mission was to occupy the area north of Pusan in order to keep the guerrillas from occupying South Korea.

At night our troops could see the movement of the guerrillas as they used hand-held lights to signal their position to other guerrilla units. In the morning, our battalion would be assigned the task of seeking out and destroying the enemy positions. Many good men never returned from those patrols.

The weeks passed and our battalion grew weary of its ever-vigilant existence.

One day, Battery Commander First Lieutenant Robert Edward Sadler informed the Unit of a show that was to be performed by a Special Service troupe. Imagine my surprise when I learned that the troupe was to be led by Dick Contino. From this day, our lives would be intertwined.

••••••••••

Dick and his troupe performing in Korea, 1953

About a month after Battery Command Lt. Sadler had informed Baker Battery of Contino's show, the troupe finally arrived at the battery position. Backed by an eleven-piece group, Contino entertained for over an hour.

After the program, as Contino and his group were preparing to travel to their next show, I rushed up to the stage to ask if he'd pose for some photos. Contino agreed and, before he knew it, most of the battery was crowding around asking to have a photo taken with the young star.

I asked Contino to sign an autograph for my wife Connie, an autograph that she treasures to this day, some forty years later.

While socializing with the soldiers, Contino caught my eye.

"Where you from, Soldier?" .

"I'm from Chicago."

Contino patted me on the shoulder and told me to look him up when he returned to the States so that we could have some pizza together.

"Hey, Bob," he told his ardent young fan, finally, "I've gotta get to my next show. I'll see you around."

"What's your hurry? You're in the Army, they can't fire you."

Laughing, the star waved good-bye.

I hated to see my idol leave. I wasn't sure what would happen. Still, something told me that our paths would cross again.

Dick meeting the troops after his performance - Bob Bove (author) standing at his left

CHAPTER TEN
BLACKLISTED

Dick was to return to the United States in the summer of 1954. He was to be honorably discharged from the Army with the rank of Staff Sergeant after receiving numerous military commendations and medals such as the Korean Defense Medal, the United Nations Medal, the American Defense Medal, the Good Conduct Medal, and the Korean Presidential Unit Citation. While returning to the United States aboard the U. S. S. Gordon, Dick headlined a show performing for other returning GI's. On the voyage, he met Fred Diodati, a young soldier from the south Philadelphia neighborhood that had spawned the great film and operatic tenor, Mario Lanza, and many other Italian-American entertainers. The young man told Dick that before he was drafted he had dreamed of being a singer. He spoke to Dick about appearing on the show.

"I listened to Fred sing and thought he had a wonderful way with a song," Dick said. "I arranged for him to appear on the program and encouraged him to give professional singing a try."

As it turned out, Contino had a sharp eye and an ear for talent. In a short while, Diodati would join The Four Aces as a vocalist and, later, would replace Al Alberts as the group's lead singer, reaping phenomenal success with such classic recordings as "Three Coins In The Fountain," "Brazil," "Tell Me Why," and, of course, "Love Is A Many Splendored Thing."

Returning home with an honorable discharge after having

served two years in the Army (sixteen months in Korea), Dick decided to continue his association with the military by volunteering to serve a six-year term in a reserve unit.

"I thought that, in some small way, making such a commitment would help erase the troubles I'd had before the war — that it would help 'pay my dues,'" Dick remembers.

Dick looked forward to his life's returning to normal and hoped that his career would return to its previous heights. However, he soon learned that the press, a press that had been so eager to publicize his problems with Uncle Sam, had not followed up on his tour of duty in the Army and that the majority of Americans were unaware of the service he had rendered to his country.

Dick was stunned by the reception he received. He had trouble in getting bookings in major rooms and clubs. It was as though he were blacklisted. Try as he might, he couldn't find anyone who'd give him a chance to prove himself or to even to listen to his story.

The more he struggled to get bookings, the more depressed he became.

After one of Dick's performance at a small California club, Frank Sinatra approached him.

"Hey, Paisan," Sinatra said, "how'd you like to play The Mocambo for a few days?"

"The Mocambo!!" Contino couldn't believe his ears.

"Hey, Frank," Dick said, "that would be great!

Here he was, unable to get bookings in rooms in small towns and Sinatra's offering him a gig at one of the premier show clubs in the world.

Sinatra wasn't kidding. Renowned for the assistance that he offered down-on-their-luck entertainers, the man known as "The Voice" was intent on helping Contino return to the spotlight. Staking Dick to a large sum of money —with no strings attached — to help him get on his feet, Sinatra was opening doors that Dick thought would remain closed forever.

"I never told Frank just how much his assistance and friendship meant to me," Dick laments. "I don't know why I never was able to say thank you for all that he did, but even now, many years later, I have never forgotten his kindness."

Several weeks after meeting Sinatra, Dick appeared at The Mocambo to the great acclaim of the public and the critics alike. Doors that had been closed for years opened as if by magic. Many celebrities crowded into the club to welcome the young genius back to the show-business fraternity.

"It was as if the bad times had never occurred," Dick smiles. "The adulation, the cheers, the friendship, everything was as it had been before the trouble."

Dick, it seemed, was on his way.

CHAPTER ELEVEN

DICK'S BETTER HALF

Still walking on air after his triumph at The Macombo, Dick began to secure bookings at prestigious clubs throughout the Hollywood area. Dick especially remembers his performances at the legendary Ciro's. The club was the premier gathering place for filmdom's leading producers, directors and stars, as well as a haunt for some of Southern California's most infamous underworld characters. At every performance, the stars would gather to appreciate the talents of the man whom Horace Heidt had called "the Valentino of the Accordion."

While Dick performed in southern California, he became a fixture in the columns written by Hedda Hopper, a former movie star who had become the single most powerful spokesperson for the entertainment world. Hopper's articles appeared in newspapers and magazines all across the country. At every opportunity, she would write with affection of the young virtuoso calling him one of the most talented entertainers in the world.

"For whatever the reason," Dick remembers, "Miss Hopper was always most gracious in writing about me. She always praised my performances and, like the town criers of old, she would dutifully report on the starlets whom I was dating at the time."

The girls whose names appeared with Dick's in Hopper's columns included Rita Moreno, Ann Blythe, Terry Moore, Gloria DeHaven, Debbie Reynolds, Anna Maria Alberghetti, and his good friend, Piper Laurie.

Once, while dating Debbie Reynolds, Dick brought her home to meet his parents. After having a wonderful Italian dinner — consisting of antipasto, giblets, salad, spaghetti and meatballs, roast chicken, potatoes, and home-made bread — Debbie began to entertain her hosts by singing and dancing throughout the house. Mama Contino didn't know what was happening, she was dumbfounded that Debbie would jump on the tables and sofas and sang numbers from "Singing In The Rain."

By the time that the performance was over and things had returned to normal, it was too late for the starlet to go home. It was decided that Reynolds would spend the night at the Contino home, strictly chaperoned, of course.

Early the next morning, Mama Contino went to the room where Reynolds was staying to awaken her for breakfast. She was shocked, though, to find that Reynolds was gone.

"Dick, Dick, Figlio," she cried, "Debbie's gone! She's not in her room!"

Dick jumped from his bed to comfort his frantic mother.

"Mama," he said, "don't worry, we'll find her — she's got to be somewhere."

After searching the house and finding no trace of the starlet, Dick jumped into his car and began to drive around the area. A few blocks from his house, Dick found Reynolds casually strolling down the street.

"Hey, Debbie," he called, "where have you been? You scared the heck out of my mother! She's frantic — sure that somebody's kidnapped you."

Reynolds, laughing, explained that she was an early riser and that she liked to walk in the morning.

"Walk?" Dick asked, shaking his head, "Walk? Just walk

over to this car so we can get home before my mom goes crazy."

Needless to say, that was Reynolds last visit to the Contino house.

Later, Dick dated Terry Moore, the beautiful pin-up queen of the Korean War. That relationship ended, however, when Howard Hughes told Moore to end the affair.

"When I heard that Mr. Hughes had told Terry to stop seeing me I knew that it would be in my best interest not to see her any longer," Dick says. "Although our romance cooled, Terry and I continued to be good friends."

While riding the crest of success in Los Angeles, Dick occasionally traveled to New York City where he would perform at private parties given by some of the country's most famous mobsters. It was at this time that Dick made the acquaintance of another show business legend, the much beloved "Schnozzola," Jimmy Durante.

"Jimmy was thinking of changing his act when we met," Dick recalls, "and, at a party on a gangster's yacht, he asked me if I'd consider touring with him as his opening act."

Although impressed with the request, Dick refused. Dick realized that taking Durante up on his offer would affect the relationship between Jimmy and his longtime partner, Eddie Jackson.

"To work with Durante, a star revered throughout the world of show business would have been a fantastic experience," Dick admitted later, "but I just couldn't do it."

Dick remembers that, whenever he appeared on the East Coast, calls would come in requesting his presence at parties and shows.

"I knew that I would have to entertain wherever I went but, what the hell, I had a great time and I got to meet some fabulous people.

What always fascinated Dick was the unusual relationship between the Mafiosi and the women they attracted — their molls.

No matter the situation, the women clung to the mobsters, acting on their every whim. As soon as a drink was finished, a fresh one would appear. If one of the men took out a cigarette, a girl would rush to his side to light it.

"Man," Dick sighs, "I thought stars had a way with women but, believe me, they had nothing on these guys."

Once, Dick remembers, he took his father along to one of the parties. Papa Contino struck up a friendship with several of the mobsters in attendance at the party and, building a relationship upon their mutual Sicilian ancestry, a "Mafioso" told Dick to "take your Dad to any store in Manhattan and get him whatever that he likes."

Dick, his father and a bodyguard supplied by their "friends," went to the city and his father had a field day picking out suits, shirts, ties, shoes — whatever caught his fancy.

"Of all the things that happened that day, Dick remembers best the cashmere overcoat that his father was taken with.

"My dad saw this beautiful coat," Dick recalls, "and, bless his soul, he just had to have it. He was a little concerned about the price — it was an astronomical amount — and he looked at me as if to question whether or not it was too expensive."

At that instant, though, the bodyguard stepped forward and, as if sensing the old man's question, took control of the situation.

"Hey, Papa Contino," he said quietly, "you like this coat? Don't worry what it costs — Mr. C _____ said that you was to have whatever you wanted so just take it."

When it came time to leave the store, the bodyguard took the selected items to the register, peeled off some bills, and carried the packages over to Dick and his father.

"My dad never got over that day," Dick recalls with a laugh, "he thought that he'd died and gone to heaven."

"For a long time after that, no matter what the temperature, you'd find pop wearing his cashmere coat."

••••••••••

Soon after his New York adventure, Dick turned his sights towards the burgeoning oasis of fun and entertainment in the Nevada desert. Only a few years before, Las Vegas had been little more than a rest stop in the desert. But, in the span of

Dick and his father, Peter, performing at a party in Glendale, California, 1954

several years, nurtured by the guidance and vision of famed underworld kingpin, Benjamin "Bugsy" Siegel, Vegas had begun to change the face of the entertainment industry in the United States. With its anything-goes atmosphere, its high stakes gambling, and its top of the line entertainment, Las Vegas became a favorite vacation spot for many of the movers and shakers of the business and entertainment worlds.

Dick readily agreed to appear at the Tropicana Hotel, one of the city's pre-eminent nightspots, and was excited about the opportunity.

While performing there, Dick began to encounter hostile audiences that openly belittled him as a "slacker." Confused, Dick went on with his performances. The heckling, however, continued.

"I couldn't believe what I was hearing," Dick recalls. "People were calling me a draft-dodging bum and a Dago slacker. They would get a few drinks in them and things would get even worse."

Dick was crushed. He'd served in the military, including a stint in Korea, and yet these people wouldn't give him the chance to entertain them.

The problem faced by Dick stemmed from the newspaper's careless reporting of his life following his trial for draft dodging. As far as most people knew, Dick had skirted military service. Much of the public imagined that while others were suffering the pain and agony of a brutal war, Dick was safe and warm surrounded by luxury.

"For whatever reason," Dick says, "the papers never reported my service during the war. The people were never told that I had served in Korea, or that President Truman had issued me a full pardon for my perceived crime. In fact, the $10,000 fine that had been issued in conjunction with my jail sentence, had been returned to me by a grateful president."

Although Dick continued to wear a happy face while performing, the constant cry of, "draft dodging bum," left a scar on the young man's psyche.

••••••••

Returning to the safety of his Hollywood sanctuary, Dick continued to perform at local clubs and to date some of Tinseltown's most beautiful women. He had long ago given up on an ambition formed during his high school years of becoming a priest. In between stints on the accordion, he modeled. It was his modeling which would bring an end to his bachelor days.

Dick on a night out

Hollywood was never short on parties and one day Dick received a telegram from Janet Leigh and her husband, Tony Curtis. It was an invitation to attend a party that the couple was throwing in honor of ladies' man Rory Calhoun who was bursting with unbridled energy on the Hollywood scene. The only problem for Dick was he had no one to take. He was dating so many ladies that he didn't want to have to choose one. He knew that he and his date would hit the Hollywood papers and he didn't want to stir up his current circle of movie starlets. He reasoned it would be better to take an unknown. Besides, it would add a bit of mystery to the social scene.

Dick thought of his good friend, the vivacious Rae Lynn of Movie Star Parade Magazine. She would know of all the up-and-coming starlets. Dick asked her to arrange a blind date for him. She said she'd think about it and get back to him.

It didn't take Lynn long to hit upon the idea of calling Leigh Snowden. She was impressed by Snowden, not because she was beautiful because Hollywood starlets all were beautiful. It was Snowden's small-town Southern charm and her inner radiance which she knew Dick would not be able to resist.

Fortunately, she reached Snowden on the first ring. When she explained the purpose of her call, Snowden asked more about her blind date. Being a singer herself, Snowden appreciated the fact that he was a musician. When Rae Lynn told her what a decent man he was, Snowden agreed to go as his date. Besides, Snowden knew both Tony Curtis and Janet Leigh since they were in Universal Studio's Freshman Class.

Lynn had told me that Leigh was an absolutely beautiful woman. But nothing could have prepared me for the sight of this lovely creature.

Hearing her footsteps on the balcony above where he stood, Dick's eyes moved to the top of the stairs.

Leigh Snowden Contino publicity photo

"The first thing I saw were the most perfect and beautiful legs that God had ever created."

As Snowden walked down the stairs, Dick's heart began to beat so fast that he was afraid she would be able to hear.

"I had seen many beautiful women in Hollywood," Dick says, "and I dated my share, too. But, as Leigh Snowden walked down the stairs, I knew that she was something special - I sensed that her beauty was not superficial, but, rather, that she had a heart and soul to match her magnificent appearance."

Like the thunderbolt that would strike Michael Corleone in "The Godfather," Dick, too was stricken. He knew that he would make this woman his wife.

Dick and Leigh dated for the last several months of 1955. On one of their dates, she told Dick that they were destined. She related the story of how she had seen Dick's poster just the day before Rae Lynn had called her. She and her good friend Barbara Stuart had been shopping in Beverly Hills when they noticed the poster Dick had posed for. Without hesitation, she had told Stuart that she was going to marry the man on the poster. She told Dick that she could hardly hold back her surprise when she saw him from the balcony — the face of the man on the poster.

Leigh's agent and others warned her that marriage at this point in her career might prove to be disastrous. Leigh had worked hard to get to where she was. While living in Covington, Tennessee, she had studied voice, drama, dancing, and the piano. By the time she reached her teens, she had begun to model. Once she had built up modeling credits, she decided to take the plunge and head west. She continued to model in San Francisco and Los Angeles. While on a modeling assignment, she met another model, Barbara Stuart. It was Stuart who had tipped her friend as to a special Armed Services show being produced by Jack Benny. Leigh auditioned and got a small walk-on part. Although Benny wasn't supposed to notice Leigh's beautiful figure, the service men did. Leigh sauntered across the stage to the appreciative whistles and cheers of the assemble multitude. The comedian, ever a consummate master of timing, pretended not to notice what was happening and, only when the roar of the service men hit a crescendo, did he turn to gaze at the gorgeous lady who had literally stopped the show.

Another problem surfaced which threatened to curtail the couple's wedding plans.

Dick's parents, like most Italian-Americans, were staunch Roman Catholics.

"Although they admitted that Leigh was a beautiful, talented and wonderful girl," Dick recalls, "they frowned on our getting married because Leigh had been divorced."

Gathering his strength, Dick faced his parents' objections telling them that, although he loved and respected them, he was in love with Leigh and that he was going to marry her.

"For the first time in my life," Dick remembers, "I was going against the wishes of my parents. Although I loved them with all of my heart, the love that I felt for Leigh was such that I couldn't let her get away."

The next day, Dick asked Leigh to marry him. She agreed and a November wedding was planned.

Soon, however, dark clouds began to appear on the horizon. The president of Universal Studios, who was busy grooming Leigh as the next blonde bombshell, told her that, because of Dick's troubles with the draft and the subsequent trial and jail sentence, she had jeopardized her career by becoming involved with him.

"Leigh stood by me," Dick remembers, "and told the people at the studios that she loved me, that she placed me above stardom, and that she would sacrifice her career, if that was what was necessary."

Leigh's loyalty to Dick had a profound effect on the Contino family. Acknowledging the character and grace of the woman who was about to become their daughter through marriage, Mama and Papa Contino embraced Leigh warmly.

The plans for the November wedding were changed when Dick was booked to appear in Hawaii for two weeks in

September. Deciding that the beautiful Hawaiian Islands would be an idyllic honeymoon spot, the wedding was moved ahead.

On Saturday, September 18, 1956, at a lavish wedding at The Beverly Hills Hotel, Dick and Leigh became man and wife. Dick's brother, Victor, served as Best Man, while Leigh's faithful friend, Barbara Stuart was Maid of Honor. The many celebrities in attendance cheered the loving couple as they escaped to their honeymoon paradise.

Although many cynics snickered at Leigh's decision, her marriage to Dick became one of the most successful in show business, lasting twenty-seven years and producing three lovely children, Mary, Deidre and Peter.

CHAPTER TWELVE
HERE'S HOLLYWOOD

Returning from the honeymoon engagement in Hawaii, Dick and Leigh moved into a beautiful home in Tarzana, California. The five-bedroom, white stucco ranch-style home with a big backyard proved to be an ideal base of operations since the majority of Dick's performances were in the Los Angeles area.

In the months following their marriage, Dick's career was on the rise. In addition to his appearances at Ciro's and other top-line clubs, he also released some recordings on the RCA, Mercury, Hamilton, and Dot labels. On several of these albums, Peter Contino, Dick's father, joined his son in performing various classic tunes such as "Che La Luna" and "El Rancho Grande." On others, Dick's wife, Leigh, showcased her singing ability by providing some beautiful vocals.

These records, coupled with Dick's regular appearances on "The Ed Sullivan Show," rekindled interest in the career of "The Adonis of the Accordion."

Hollywood, too, began to knock at Dick's door. His first effort as an actor was his appearance on the famous Lux Video Theatre. The program, a remake of the renowned Dana Andrews - Merle Oberon classic film, "Night Song," featured Dick as a blind pianist. Co-starring with Dick was the achingly beautiful Barbara Rush.

"The thing I'll always remember about the show," Dick says, "was Barbara's kindness and sensitivity. She became so involved in the story that she literally cried at some of the script's tender moments."

"The whole Lux Theatre experience was uplifting, and working with Barbara was one of the happiest times of my life."

In short order, Dick moved on to two independent films. He starred in "Daddy-O" and "Big Night." Although he did the best he could, Dick was unable to overcome the "B" quality scripts and amateurish production values that hounded each project.

While working hard to improve his acting ability, Dick found an excellent teacher in his wife, Leigh, had worked with such Hollywood stars as Donald O'Connor, Jim Backus, Rock Hudson, Janet Leigh, Tony Curtis, and a tall, thin youngster whom some predicted would have no future in Hollywood — Clint Eastwood.

"Leigh was a fantastic acting coach," Dick recalls. "She would give me hints on ways of expressing myself, ways of understanding that the exaggerated movements that worked so well on a nightclub or auditorium stage had no place in film. The camera is a subtle instrument, one that best reveals talent in a quiet, almost transparent way."

"I know it sounds easy, but, believe me, acting was, probably, the hardest work that I'd ever done."

Snowden's coaching and expertise in the acting art paid off when Dick was approached by representatives of Metro-Goldwyn-Mayer Studios — "The Home of More Stars Than There Are In Heaven" — to star in a film entitled "Girl's Town."

The film co-starred sex-goddess Mamie Van Doren, Mel Torme, Paul Anka, Ray Anthony, Maggie Hayes, Kathy Crosby, and The Platters. It was directed by Charles Haas. The

Dick and Leigh performing at the Monee Auction, 1980

Dick with his beautiful wife, Leigh

plot revolved around a wild young girl (Van Doren) who was sent to a reform school for young women where she learned that she wasn't as smart or as tough as she thought she was.

Although it will never be mistaken for a classic, the years since the film's release have seen it garner quite a cult following.

Dick played Van Doren's boyfriend in the picture. Although he had a ball with Mel Torme, Paul Anka, Ray Anthony, and The Platters, he realized that his first love was performing on stage.

After completing "Girl's Town," Dick ended his flirtation with the movies.

In the late fifties, appearing with Leigh as his vocal guest star, Dick attempted to right his career. Dick and Leigh played nightclubs and showrooms across the country. Because of her close friendship with Art Linkletter, the pair eventually was booked to appear on Linkletter's highly-rated television show.

"Leigh thought that appearing on television would help open doors to bigger and better bookings," says Dick, "but things didn't work out."

Once again, Dick traveled to Las Vegas to play engagements at The Tropicana, The Flamingo, The Frontier, and The Sahara. With Leigh was at his side, as Dick again faced hostility from a small portion of the audience at almost every show. Cries of "You lousy slacker!," or "You draft dodgin' piece of scum!" could be heard at almost every Contino performance. Dick's audiences grew smaller and smaller and, although he had steeled himself for the heckling that he knew was inevitable, Leigh became distraught at the unfair treatment heaped upon her man. Things became so upsetting, that Dick, aware of the strain being placed upon his wife, began to seek comfort in the bottle.

"Things deteriorated to such an extent that Leigh would bring my discharge papers to the shows," Dick recalls. "Many times she would confront the people belittling me, show them my discharge papers, and question the reason for their mistreatment of me."

Uncomfortable with the situation, Dick began to drink and gamble. Dick, who had always been a moderate drinker, now consumed vast quantities of liquor. Even worse, he began to frequent the gambling tables and, as might be expected, would lose heavily. Dick estimates that he gambled away a quarter of a million dollars.

The lowest point in these troublesome times came on an

evening when Dick drank and gambled away $10,000 while Leigh stood by, unable to help the man that she loved.

"I had the fever that night," Dick sadly remembers, "craps, cards, roulette — I tried them all. I kept losing more and more and Leigh, though she never said a word, was visibly upset."

Finally, with his money gone and his credit exhausted, Dick turned to Leigh for solace.

Gathering the dignity that never abandoned her, Leigh drew herself erect and stared into her husband's eyes.

"Alright, you son of a bitch," the beauty coldly said, "you've made an ass of yourself and you've lost all of our money — now are you satisfied?"

The remark shamed Dick and he became embarrassed; he had never before heard Leigh swear.

Slowly, he raised his eyes, expecting Leigh to continue her verbal attack. Instead, she extended her arms, understanding that Dick was battling demons that could not be exorcised in a single night.

"Come on, Daddy" she said, "let's go home."

CHAPTER THIRTEEN

ON THE WAGON

Trying to get his life in order, Dick acquired a new agent who would secure bookings in small towns across America. But, the demon pursued him.

Though he tried, Dick found that he couldn't perform without drinking. It had become nothing for him to consume a fifth of whiskey before going on-stage.

"I traveled with a bottle of booze in my accordion case," Dick remembers. "I played several engagements and, because of the booze, couldn't remember the show."

Once, while visiting his parents, Dick's mother discovered the liquor in his case.

"Figlio," she asked, "que fa (what are you doing)?"

Embarrassed, Dick told his mother that a friend had given him the liquor as a gift.

"She didn't say anything," he remembers, "but I knew that she knew I was lying."

••••••••••

Recalling those times, Dick says that the only good thing he did while lost in drink was to write an arrangement for "The Battle Hymn of the Republic," an arrangement that, to this day, he uses as the finale for each show. Miraculously, Dick had also completed an arrangement for "Exodus," one of the most popular tunes of the day.

"I woke up with a terrible hangover and noticed sheet music crumpled beneath my arm. I looked at the two arrangements and, sight reading them, I was amazed at what I'd done while I was drunk. I took out my accordion, played the songs, and was shocked at how good they were. I swear, I don't know how the arrangements were done."

While continuing his tour, Dick was accompanied by a pianist, a marvelous musician. Not surprisingly, in addition to his musical expertise the pianist could match Dick drink for drink.

The pair continued their travels. As the days rolled into weeks, the alcoholic haze surrounding the duo worsened.

"One day in Mexico City," Dick recalls," the pianist turned to me and raised his shaking hands. He told me he couldn't take it anymore — that he 'was going on the wagon.' I didn't believe him."

To Dick's amazement, the man was true to his word. He quit "cold turkey." Days passed. Then weeks. Then a month. The transformation was nothing short of remarkable. Hands that could never be still, suddenly hung quietly at his sides. The musician appeared more relaxed and looked physically improved.

The change in his friend had a startling effect on Dick as well.

"I figured, what the hell, if he could do it, then I could, too."

From that day, Dick never took another drink.

•••••••••

It was at about this time, while Dick was battling the bottle, that he got a call from his wife — a call that would have a terrible impact on the couple's life.

Leigh had gone shopping and had written a check to cover the purchases. Later she learned that the check had been rejected for insufficient funds. She called Dick who was amazed at the turn of events. He reminded Leigh that he had never handled the money and that his agents were in charge of his financial affairs.

He thought that the bank had made an error. For a long while, Dick's talent agency had been entrusted with his money. Dick couldn't believe that the agency could have done anything wrong.

On the heels of this news, Dick called his friend, Wayne Newton, and told him what had happened. Newton told Dick, with sadness in his voice, that the agent took his money also.

"Dick, it's true," Newton said. "They owe you thousands of dollars, but, you'll just have to stand in line — hell, they took me for over two hundred grand."

Newton explained that the agents had squandered the money and told Dick that there was no point in trying to recoup his losses.

"Hell," he said, "they haven't got a dime left. You and I, well, we'll just have to start all over again."

Dick couldn't believe what Newton had told him. His worst fears had been realized. The men had embezzled money to such an extent that he was plunged into desperate financial straits.

Faced with the embezzlement, Dick had no choice. He filed for bankruptcy.

Although losing their beautiful home in Tarzana and other valuable possessions was difficult for Dick and Leigh, the couple faced the future together. They knew that, no matter what, they'd always have each other and their wonderful children. Their love would see them through.

After discussing things with Leigh, the couple decided to move to Fresno. Dick would be going "home."

CHAPTER FOURTEEN
THE ROAD BACK

Moving back to Fresno was difficult for Dick. He'd left home a conquering hero and now, little more than a decade later, he'd returned as a prodigal son. The fame and fortune he had achieved were all but gone. Many of the friends he'd made in the past ten years had disappeared. But his family was there to provide him with love. His home-town friends assured him that he wasn't alone in his fears.

Although he played an occasional gig, Dick couldn't muster the enthusiasm that once had come so naturally.

Dick's shows, although well-received in his hometown area, couldn't provide the entertainer with the lift he had grown to expect while playing the "big" rooms in Vegas and Hollywood. The support that old friends offered, while deeply appreciated, couldn't satisfy Dick's desire to return to the position of prominence he had once held.

"After each show I couldn't wait to return home to Leigh," Dick recalls. "There, in the comfort of her arms, I found the strength and support that I needed."

He realized that he would have to forsake the comfort and security of Fresno, if he were to regain his stardom and, more importantly, earn a livelihood that would support his loving wife and family. Dick suggested to Leigh that they should move to Las Vegas.

Leigh agreed. She realized that staying in Fresno would further debilitate Dick. Even though Las Vegas held no promises, the couple believed that their situation would improve. The many showrooms in the city combined with Dick's reputation as one of the hardest-working men in show business would give them a better chance at re-gathering their lives.

A short time later, the Contino family moved to Las Vegas. There, calling upon contacts that Dick had made in the past years, he was able to secure bookings in several clubs. Playing mainly at The Tropicana, Dick established a reputation as a steady and dependable showman — someone who could be depended upon to provide an outstanding evening's entertainment.

"While I played my gigs," Dick says, "I would be heckled on occasion. But, call it mellowing out, or call it maturity, I handled that problem better than I had before."

"Don't get me wrong — it hurt to have to suffer the barbs and wisecracks that came my way. The people gave me the same old garbage about the draft, but I had served my country proudly."

Many times Dick wondered where all the men were that he had entertained in Korea. Where were the men that he had served with? Why didn't someone take a stand? He was convinced that, of all the thousands of soldiers that he had entertained in Korea, surely some of them must have been in attendance at a show where he was being heckled. Why didn't some of them come to his defense?

Dick continued to perform, with his beloved Leigh being the only one who would leap to his defense.

"She was my rock," Dick says. "Without her, I would have been nothing."

Performing steadily, Dick managed to earn enough money to purchase a beautiful home in Las Vegas. The white stucco, bi-level home located on a quiet cul-de-sac had belonged to Vito Musso, a well-known saxophonist with The Stan Kenton Orchestra.

Dick and Leigh struggled to turn their newly-purchased house into a home. The couple happily wandered through many stores seeking the furniture and accessories that would help to make the house a perfect refuge for the couple and their five children. Little by little, things improved.

Dick remembers a funny thing about that house.

"One day, when I had returned from an appearance, Peter, my youngest son, told me, 'Hey, Dad, there's some guy who keeps coming into our yard and stealing our vegetables.' The next day, I solved the mystery."

Early the next morning, Dick saw Musso coming into the yard. As he watched from the kitchen window, he saw Musso walk to the garden. Like many Italians, Musso had planted a garden in his back yard to grow his own vegetables. As he picked some tomatoes, Dick confronted him. "Hey, Vito, what's goin' on? You're scaring the hell out my son, walking in here and taking tomatoes from the garden."

The older man looked at Dick. He stood silently for a long while. He glanced at the tomatoes, then back at Dick.

"Listen, Dick," he finally said, "I may have sold you my house, but I'm claiming visitation rights to the garden. Until I can plant another, get used to seeing me here because I'll be a regular customer."

Dick remembers the laughter that came from both men — laughter that was loud enough to awaken the entire household.

CHAPTER FIFTEEN
TO RUSSIA, WITH LOVE

During the 1960's, Dick, although playing many clubs in Las Vegas, did most of his entertaining at The Tropicana. While performing in Vegas, he continued his excellent working relationship with television's legendary Ed Sullivan.

Sullivan, the former New York newsman had parlayed his knowledge of the entertainment world and an ability for discovering talent into a legendary show business career. It was Sullivan who had first booked Dick immediately after the youngster had won the championship on Horace Heidt's Original Youth Program in 1948. At that time, Sullivan's program was a regional television broadcast, serving the northeastern United States. As the years passed, the show had gone national. "Toast of the Town" became a top-rated program. Its popularity lasted for nearly a quarter century. For many families, the program became a ritualistic experience — Sunday dinner and the Sullivan Show were a staple of the American diet.

Dick appeared regularly on Sullivan's program. Each appearance added to his legion of fans. Eventually, Dick would appear on the program a record forty eight times.

Following Dick's discharge from the Army, each time he appeared on Sullivan's program, the sonorous voice always introduced Dick as "The Michaelangelo of the Accordion, Staff Sergeant Dick Contino."

"Mr. Sullivan would always, without fail, publicly recognize my service to my country," Dick recalls with affection.

"He was one of the few media personalities who did so."

While others made no attempt to make it known that Dick had fulfilled his service obligation, prompting much of the heckling and harassment that came my way, Sullivan always defended Dick and offered him a spot on his program.

The friendship that existed between the showman and the accordionist grew as the years passed.

John F. Kennedy was in the White House. The Cold War had escalated to a near fever pitch. Russian bases in Cuba and Soviet intervention in Africa, Central America and Viet Nam would bring the world to the brink of a nuclear holocaust. It was then that the United States State Department contacted Sullivan with an interesting proposal.

"The government asked Sullivan his thoughts about a 'Cultural Exchange' program with the Soviet Union," Dick notes. "The idea was to bring a troupe of American entertainers to Russia to promote good will between the two nations."

Sullivan accepted the challenge and went about gathering a troupe that would represent the United States — "The Greatest Country on Earth" — during a four week tour of the Soviet Union.

When the impresario asked him to join the troupe, Dick could hardly believe his ears. How could he, a man who had been maligned for his troubles with the military, be asked to represent his country — to bring a slice of Americana to a foreign shore. The irony was not wasted on Dick.

"I told Mr. Sullivan that I would be thrilled to go." The tour would be an ideal opportunity to serve his country again — as he had done in the Korean War. He definitely looked forward to the challenge.

Another benefit of the tour would be the psychological lift of appearing before a non-judgmental audience. It was a

Dick posing with Petosa Accordion, 1964. Seattle, Washington

chance to play before people who would appreciate his ability on an instrument that was beloved throughout the Soviet world.

"As hard as it is to admit," Dick says, "I welcomed the opportunity to play before foreign audiences, to entertain people who would respect my talent and who wouldn't hurl obscenities and vitriol my way."

"Although I had become used to the harassment that would come my way during many performances, I was relieved to have the chance to perform before a polite and knowledgeable public."

Just before leaving to take part in the exchange, Dick began his relationship with Petosa Accordions. Located in Seattle, Washington, the Petosa company had been custom-crafting accordions since 1922. Dick, a stickler for the quality of his instruments, was pleased to become associated with the company.

"I happened to get in touch with Joe Petosa one day because I was having problems with accordions breaking down," Dick recalls. "I told him that I was tired of keys sticking and bellows bursting and asked if he had an accordion that could stand up to the rigors of my performances."

Assured by Petosa that such an accordion could be made available, Dick took the Artist's Model -1100 on a trial basis.

"It was the best move I ever made," Dick says.

The model that Dick used and continues to use is the Artist's Model -1100. The completely handmade accordion takes up to one year to build and costs $10,000.00. With reeds crafted of the finest Swedish blue steel, and covered with leather of the finest calfskin, a keyboard and bellows made of American walnut aged over twenty years, a tone chamber constructed of a solid piece of Honduras Mahogany, and a bass mechanism individually made and fitted to achieve precision and very fine tolerances. Dick feels that the AM-1100 is the finest accordion in the world.

Before flying to Moscow, the troupe attended a party that was given by the State Department. That evening, as the music and laughter flowed, Leigh, who had agreed to accompany her husband on the trip, shared old memories with friends such as dancers Marge and Gower Champion. They also spent some time meeting members of the tour whom they hadn't before met. Among these new friends was Contralto Risé Stevens. The party was a great success and the excitement of sharing the adventure of the tour with both new and old friends made Dick feel like a new person.

While preparing for the tour, Dick was concerned about several aspects of the performances. Who would be the musicians that would accompany him during his performances? How would his arrangements "go over" with a new and foreign audience?

"Although music is a universal language, I was concerned about performing in such a way that would please the Soviet people," Dick recalls. "I guess that, even after years of entertaining, those were normal feelings."

The flight to Moscow was a unique and wonderful experience. When the troupe arrived in the Russian capitol, the tumultuous welcome by the Russian people thrilled the entertainers. Throngs of citizens greeted the plane when it landed. The screams of adulation brought back memories of Dick's days as a teen idol.

Meeting with Soviet dignitaries and attending lunches, dinners and press meetings with governmental officials in charge of the exchange gave Dick a new perspective on the Soviet nation.

"The Russian people were warm and friendly," Dick remembers. "I, like many of the entertainers, had never met a citizen of the Soviet Union — all that I knew of the country was what I had heard about on the news or read in the American newspapers."

What Dick discovered was a country inhabited by a friendly and gracious people. The Soviet citizens had a special place in their hearts for entertainers — people that they considered to be artists of the first magnitude.

Dick had never realized that Russian entertainers were treated like royalty. The country, like all countries, had endured its share of pain, suffering and problems. But, the people, even though they understood the preferential treatment afforded their entertainers, showed no animosity towards them.

"I guess that the escape that the entertainment provided, the chance to see talented women and men perform the works of Chekov or Tchaikovsky or to listen to such popular classics as 'Dark Eyes' and 'The Volga Boatman' did wonders in helping the people forget the pain and misery of their existence," Dick mused.

Soon after arriving in Russia, rehearsals for the shows began. The worries that had plagued Dick concerning the quality of his "back-up" musicians vanished when, to his amazement, he learned that he would be performing in Moscow and Leningrad with one of the world's great orchestras — The Moscow Symphony.

"I was in shock," Dick recalls. "The Moscow Symphony! I mean, geez, no offense intended, but that wasn't like playing with some small town band. This was the big time!"

The musicians of the symphony arrived for the first rehearsal and, Dick admits, his nerves were aflutter. Soon, though, he felt at ease.

During meetings with the symphony's conductor, they discussed many things; things of the world and, of course, the music that Dick would play — tunes such as "Around The World In Eighty Days," "The Beer Barrel Polka" and "The Contino Boogie." While handing out copies of the arrangements, Dick was pleased to notice the friendly, yet businesslike, attitude that pervaded the orchestra. The musicians, dressed in top-of-the-line clothes, seemed to appreciate their prestigious status. But, although a formality was inherent in the proceedings, the warmth of the people, especially when working on our music, gave Dick a sense of camaraderie and a feeling of comfort that he remembers to this day.

Two of the tour's shows were scheduled for Moscow's famed Gorky Park. Each show was to consist of two segments. Each entertainer could perform in either portion of the program. Due to the Soviet's love of the accordion and because of Dick's virtuosity on the instrument, it was decided that Dick would close each segment of the program.

"I was torn when Mr. Sullivan asked me to close the program's segments," recalls Dick. "I was a member of the troupe and didn't want to be singled out or to alienate the other entertainers who were part of the troupe."

Dick's concerns were allayed when Sullivan explained that the Russian people requested and in fact, demanded that Dick be the "star" of the program.

"Such was the power of the Soviet's love of the accordion," Dick remembers with a smile, "that I was singled out for the closing segments of the show."

Meeting and talking with the conductor and members of The Moscow Symphony provided Dick with another surprise. It was suggested, time and again, that Dick remain in the Soviet Union after the exchange was ended. They suggested that he become a Soviet citizen. Dick was told that, should he choose to become a "Soviet" entertainer, he would become a legend in the country and would assume the icon-like status that was reserved for the greatest performers in the land.

"I thought that they were kidding me about staying behind," recalls Dick. "I went along with their jokes, but, when they told me that I would never have to worry about expenses, or money, or education for my children, or a place to live, or status as a pre-eminent citizen — well, then I knew that they were serious."

As gracefully as he could, Dick let it be known that, although he would miss his cheering and respectful fans and that he hoped to return to perform for the Russian people, he intended to remain in the United States.

"Although I was ostracized by many in America ... although many of the major stars, producers, showrooms, and studios in the United States blacklisted me, I could not turn my back on the country that I loved."

Following the amazing success of the performances in Moscow and Leningrad, the troupe returned home.

Later, in conversation with his father, Dick would casually discuss the offer to move to Russia. Papa Contino told Dick that, while he certainly didn't want to live in the Soviet Union, he might want to consider moving to Europe where entertainers were revered. There, he reminded his son, accordion players were afforded a respect not found in the United States. In the final analysis, Dick would not uproot his family to pursue dreams of glory in a foreign land.

From the heights of success ... from the adulation of thousands upon thousands of knowledgeable music fans ... from offers of financial and personal security for himself and his family so that he could return to the land of his birth, Dick was about to change his course and embark upon a series of engagements that would be far removed from the magnificent experience of the trip to the Soviet Union.

CHAPTER SIXTEEN
BIDING HIS TIME

In stark contrast to the magical experience in Russia was Dick's first engagement back home at a casino in Elko, Nevada, far removed from the adoring thousands in Gorky Park. Dick was greeted by a group of cowboys standing in sheep manure and tossing silver dollars into the slot machines.

Dick found himself entertaining in a small lounge.

"I was depressed, especially after returning from such a wonderful experience in Russia, but, as a showman, I never hesitated in giving the audience my best shot."

Other engagements followed. Dick continued performing across the country. Although he continued to give an excellent performance wherever he played, Dick was restricted to small clubs. The "big rooms" that he so desperately wanted to play remained beyond his reach.

A few times, when it looked like things were about to break for him, something always happened and things never worked out.

One of the "things" that could have turned Dick's life around was a proposed television show to be sponsored by the Singer Sewing Machine Company.

In the Sixties when "The Lawrence Welk Show" was at the height of its popularity, with much of its popularity derived from the accordion playing of Myron Floren. The General Artists Corporation of New York approached Dick about getting together a band for television.

As plans proceeded, Dick incurred a great deal of personal expense in putting together the band — expenses that included the signing of musicians to contracts, having new musical arrangements written, having stage costumes and band props created, and recording an album in preparation for the show.

To Dick's regret, however, General Artists arranged a meeting with him. He was told that the show would not be produced. The explanation was that the Singer Company had dropped out as a sponsor because of its concern about "adverse publicity."

Such reversals took their toll. Dick became more and more depressed with the way his career was going. With his beloved Leigh and his children at his side, however, he persevered.

In the late 1960's and early 1970's, Dick continued his recording career, primarily on the Mercury label. During this time he would record a total of twelve albums which garnered sales of more than six million records. Although the albums were good, they never reached — nor did Dick expect them to reach — the top of the sales charts.

He continued to make personal appearances. Occasionally, a television program would call.

"I just played the hand that I'd been dealt."

One of the television programs that called was ABC-TV's "The Joey Bishop Show." Bishop was then the main competitor to Johnny Carson's reign as the king of late night television. Dick's performance before the live audience brought down the house.

"I could feel the warmth of the audience," Dick says, "and I just knew that the performance had gone over very well."

After he played several accordion pieces, Bishop invited

Dick to sit next to him and be interviewed. The pair spent the next few minutes engaged in some idle chatter. During a commercial break, Bishop leaned over to Dick.

"Dick, you've been done a terrible injustice. I'm gonna set the record straight tonight."

Dick was elated! Was it possible that this was the night that he'd dreamed of for so long? At long last, through the medium of television, Dick would be able to explain his story to the millions of people watching "The Joey Bishop Show."

After the break, Bishop re-introduced Dick. After a few minutes, he launched into the draft controversy.

In response to Bishop's questions, Dick reacted in the flamboyant, enthusiastic manner so often associated with his Italian heritage.

"I was waving my arms and gesturing," he recalls, "trying to say, in essence, 'What do these people want from me? I served my time in the Army and paid for any mistakes that I might have made. I mean, I did what was right for my country.'"

As the program ended, Bishop congratulated Dick on his outstanding performance.

Dick thought that he had been vindicated. He waited for calls to appear on other programs, appearances that would help propel him to the top of the show business ladder. In fact, Dick later was scheduled to appear on 'The Tonight Show with Johnny Carson. Sadly, the appearance never materialized due to a strike by the cameramen's union.

"I guess that things like that are an indication of the misfortune that seemed to follow my career," Dick says.

Frustrated by the lack of interest on Bishop's part, Dick decided to get to the bottom of the issue.

"A year goes by and Joey doesn't use me, doesn't even call

to say hello. I became more and more frustrated — I have, always have had, a difficult time accepting rejection — and decided to take matters into my own hands. I had to see just what was happening!"

Dick went to Bishop's office.

"Hey, Joey," Dick said, after the usual pleasantries were out of the way, "what's going on? A year ago I'm on your program, get a great reaction from the audience, have a wonderful interview with you, and .... a year goes by and I don't hear a word from you! What's goin' on?"

Bishop told the entertainer that some things had happened as a result of the program and that he didn't know whether to side with Dick or with the people who didn't like what Dick did."

Upon hearing this, Dick became furious, unable to understand what the comedian was saying.

"Joey," he said, "what do you mean? What the hell did I do?"

"Well, you know," Bishop shrugged, "you can't come on national television and tell off the American people. You can't tell the public, 'Hey, what do you expect from me?'"

Bishop then changed the subject, asking Dick for the real story of what happened during the draft controversy. The question exasperated Dick even more.

"Do I have to go over that again? What really happened? What really happened is that I made a mistake and paid for it. Damn, I'm still paying for it. Even if you want to call what I did a mistake, where's the forgiveness? Where's the great heart of the American people? The Japanese bombed Pearl Harbor in 1941 and the Nazi's tried to conquer the world. Did we forgive them? Damn right we did. You can find companies in every major American city controlled by Japanese or German interests — you can't help seeing signs that say Sony or Toyota or Mercedes-Benz."

"We've forgiven them," Dick concluded, "but they can't forgive me. They run companies, prospering on American soil and I can't get on a lousy television show."

Knowing that his hopes had been dashed once again, Dick left Bishop's office. He knew, then, that he would never again appear on the comedian's show.

CHAPTER SEVENTEEN
AT THE FRONT

In the wake of the Korean Conflict, the American people had hoped that armed conflict would vanish from the world. Little did they know that, while the Korean Conflict raged, an unimportant French colony in the far east, French Indochina, would, in a few short years, become the "next Korea."

American military involvement in Viet Nam began after France had abandoned the country. Communist Forces controlled the northern section of the country and, in an effort to "keep the world safe from Communism," the United States sent military troops to advise and to train the South Vietnamese army. A short time later, American lives were being lost in an undeclared war.

As the conflict raged, major American stars such as Jane Fonda and Joan Baez visited North Viet Nam to decry American involvement in a genocidal conflict. Athletes such as Muhammad Ali refused induction into the military service. The American military sought entertainers for the soldiers; to provide them a reprieve from the horrors of the war. In 1966, one of the first performers to volunteer his services was Dick Contino.

"Having been in Korea and having seen, first hand, what entertainment can mean to men who've been in combat, I felt that it was my duty to offer my services to the men."

Dick and Leigh traveled to Viet Nam as part of an entertainment troupe — the type of entertainment troupe that the legendary Bob Hope had made so famous. Dick and Leigh entertained whenever and wherever they were needed.

Once, while performing for an isolated company of Marines that had been in combat for an extensive period of time, Dick and his troupe encountered an enemy attack.

"We had to take cover as soon as the attack began," Dick recalls. "I understood the danger that we were in but, Leigh, unaccustomed to what was happening, was terrified."

"We endured the barrage for the rest of the day and, as always, my main concern was for Leigh's safety."

When darkness fell, the attack subsided and the troupe was able to be airlifted out of the combat zone.

"I was grateful to escape with my wife and our troupe intact," Dick remembers, "but I always regretted the fact that we were unable to perform for those wonderful guys."

Soon after the attack in the combat zone, Dick and his troupe were performing for another group of Marines that had been recalled from their mission in the combat zone. During the performance, someone began to heckle Dick.

Although Dick tried to ignore the man and to continue with his performance, the heckling continued.

Dick stopped the show abruptly. Looking the heckler square in the eye, he said, "Look, what you're saying is true. You'll get no beef from me. As a mixed-up kid I made a mistake, a mistake that I'm still paying for."

The Marines in the audience, the vast majority of them unfamiliar with Dick's problems with the military, began to side with the heckler. They questioned Dick's patriotism and his courage. It was then, as things were about to turn ugly, that a Non-Commissioned-Officer slowly walked onto the stage and came to Dick's defense.

"Look," the steely-eyed sergeant said as the crowd grew quiet, "you shut-up and listen to what I'm telling you. This man ... Dick Contino ... sure, he made some mistakes. We all did. But listen to me — and hear me loud and clear — he did serve in the military. I know — I was in Korea and I saw him there."

The soldiers listened to the grizzled veteran and, slowly, as the words began to sink in, they came over to Dick's side. As the entertainer continued his program, the audience was swept up in the music. At the end of each number, a chorus of cheers and encouraging shouts washed across the stage.

That was an important show for Dick. It marked the first time that someone from the military — someone with whom he'd served in Korea — had sprung to his defense."

As Dick left the stage to a deafening ovation of the GI's, tears welled in his eyes. No one, with the exception of Leigh, knew how much the Sergeant's words had meant to him.

CHAPTER EIGHTEEN
AT PEACE WITH HIMSELF

When Dick returned from Viet Nam his career fell into the same old rut. He was forced to play engagements in small towns and in small clubs. The rejection began to take its toll.

Giving his all at every show, Dick would do his best to conceal the anguish that he felt. Many times he would come off stage in a state of depression. Eventually, his family and, especially, his precious Leigh, feared for his well-being.

Like the trooper that she was, Leigh moved to help her husband take control of his life. She encouraged him to broaden his horizons, to put his frustration to good use. Although self-help had never been his cup of tea, Leigh encouraged Dick to read and to listen to psychological and philosophical tapes. The books and tapes provided good therapy for Dick and helped during his recurring periods of depression.

"Before Leigh got me interested in the books and tapes I often felt angry and depressed," remembers Dick. "The serenity and satisfaction that I found in them did wonders for me."

Another positive aspect of the new-found peace that pervaded Dick's life was the fact that he was able to overcome his contemplated return to the bottle.

"I had licked drinking once before," said Dick, referring to the days before his cold turkey cure in Mexico City, "but, occasionally, when I was performing and someone would scream some obscenity towards me, or mention something

AT PEACE WITH HIMSELF

Dick Contino

about my being a draft dodger, I must admit that there were times when a drink would have tasted awfully good."

Armed with the love of his wife and children, and with the solace afforded by his books and tapes, Dick was able to keep the temptation to return to drink at bay.

Eventually, he came to realize that he could not alter the course of his life; that he could not be anything other than what and who he was — Dick Contino.

"It was at about this time that I realized that I wasn't going to change my life overnight, that the days of the big clubs and television and the movies were finished."

"Gradually I knew that what I needed; what I'd been searching for during the lost years was my self respect — a little peace of mind."

Being able to understand what he wanted was a great turning point in Dick's life.

"I wanted to perform," Dick says. "If people wanted me to play, I'd play. I didn't care if it was a Command Performance for the Queen of England; a White House recital; a three-week stand at Carnegie Hall; or a benefit for the homeless in some small town. I didn't care, if I played for thousands of people in a crowded amphitheater or for a few people in a friend's living room. All I wanted was my peace of mind and my music."

CHAPTER NINETEEN

THE SEVENTIES

Dick faced the decade of the Seventies renewed with a peace of mind and serenity that had eluded him for years. Although it was not the "big time," he was able to play his music and to provide his family with everything that it needed.

"The early Seventies were great years for me and my family," Dick said. "I enjoyed being able to watch my children mature. The love that Leigh and I shared grew with each passing day."

Among the great joys of Dick's life was the time that he was able to spend with his children. The family loved to spend time together — picnics, hikes, games — the Contino's enjoyed them all. As the children grew, Dick and Leigh appreciated the special talents each child possessed — Mary had a beautiful voice and was considering a career in show business. Deidre had inherited her father's love for exercise and activity and everyone had to move "double time" to keep up with the young dynamo. Peter loved music and was interested in learning to play the accordion and the drums. The presence of Cathy and Robert, Leigh's children from her first marriage whom Dick had adopted, added to the joy of the family's life.

"We were like 'Ozzie and Harriet' or 'The Brady Bunch,'" Dick remembers. "All our outings were filled with love and good times and, without doubt, Leigh was the primary reason for that happiness ."

As time passed Dick began to notice that Leigh became increasingly tired and short-winded. Although she never complained, her husband saw that, at times, the sparkle that highlighted her luminescent blue eyes seemed to disappear.

One day their daughter Mary noticed a black spot on her mother's shoulder. Mary explained that at school that day, her class had learned that dark spots on the skin could be a harbinger of a cancerous growth.

Leigh laughed at her daughter's warning but, when Mary insisted that she have the spot checked, Leigh gave in and made an appointment to see the family doctor.

A few days after the visit, the family doctor called to tell Leigh that he wanted to see her. Driving to the doctor's office, Dick had a premonition about Leigh that the visit that she had consented to in such a light-hearted manner would alter their lives.

After exchanging the usual pleasantries, the physician's manner became serious. He told Dick and Leigh that Mary's fears had proven correct. The spot on Leigh's shoulder was indicative of cancer. She would require surgery as quickly as was possible.

There was no other option. Leigh needed the surgery and the arrangements were made.

Just a few short weeks after that casual family discussion, Leigh was admitted to the hospital and the surgery was performed. The operation was a success. However, the doctor warned Dick that a recurrence of the melanoma was possible.

Leigh left the hospital after a few days and, before long, was back to being her usual sparkling self.

Dick continued to work in and around the Las Vegas area. Life was pleasant.

In the mid-Seventies Dick and Leigh's daughter, Mary, was selected to represent Nevada in the prestigious Miss USA

Dick's daughter, Mary, first runner up of Miss U.S.A., 1977

competition. She finished as first runner-up, losing to Miss Texas by a scant one-quarter point. Dick and Leigh were, of course, thrilled with their girl's success.

"There were tears in our eyes," Dick remembers, "as Leigh and I watched our little girl perform during the pageant. Her grace, her beauty, her talent — she was so much like Leigh that I was shocked. She was great!"

Some time later Mary would put her talent — the talent that had been so apparent during the Miss USA Pageant — to work when she toured with her father. It would be one of the happiest times of Dick's eventful life.

CHAPTER TWENTY
WE'LL MEET AGAIN

In 1975, more than twenty years after meeting in Korea, I met Dick in Lyons, Illinois, a small town south of Chicago.

For years, my wife Connie had been telling him of Dick's appearances in the Chicagoland area. She always encouraged me to see him perform.

I brushed off my wife's suggestion, saying that Dick had extended his invitation years before and had probably done so to make a home-sick soldier feel a little bit better about the way that things were going.

Finally, after years of discussing the possibility, Connie noticed a news story concerning Dick's upcoming appearance at the Lyons Club.

Surprising my wife, I reserved tickets to the show. My excitement about seeing the great performer mounted and I decided to bring with me to the performance the photos and autograph that I had been cherishing since the Korean War.

Arriving at the club, I was surprised to find that it was nearly deserted and that my wife and I were the first patrons of the show.

A few minutes later Connie and I were approached by another couple who introduced themselves as Wally and Barbara Radicek. Anticipating the evening's show, Barbara asked me how I had come to attend the performance.

I answered that I had seen Dick when he performed for our battery in Korea. I showed the woman the photos I had taken and the autograph that Dick had signed for Connie.

Barbara, a member of the original Contino Fan Club in Chicago, questioned me as to why the Korean veterans who had been entertained by Dick during the conflict had abandoned him when he had resumed his career.

She wondered where the Korean vets where when Dick was performing in and around Chicago. Why hadn't they come to his defense when the people jeered at him and called him a 'draft dodger?'

I was taken by surprise. I told Barbara that I had no idea of the problems that Dick had endured or of the persecution he had suffered because of his troubles with the draft.

I told her that I had just assumed that Dick was doing well and that he was living the life of a "star."

Barbara went on to tell me of the hardship that Dick had faced in the years following his return from the war.

Stung by what I had heard, I asked Barbara to arrange for me see Dick in private. She told me that Dick hadn't arrived yet because he was attending a party with some members of his fan club. We continued to talk. Suddenly, Connie tapped me on the arm.

"There he is ... Dick Contino."

Barbara waved to him and, taking me by the hand she said, "Come on, let's go see the man you met in Korea."

After exchanging pleasantries, I showed Dick the photos that I had taken during the show in Korea. I called Connie to my side, introducing her as the lovely lady who had inspired me to seek his autograph all those years ago.

During an exchange of war experiences, Dick asked me to stay after the show to continue our discussion.

I was amazed that Dick seemed like such a regular guy. He was the same down-to-earth person that I had met behind the lines during the war.

After the show, I told Dick that I was disappointed at the small turnout for the show. I had expected a packed club and was upset at the small number of fans that had come to see him.

"To your credit, Dick, you put on one hell of a show."

When it came time for the performer to leave, Dick mentioned that he would soon be returning to the Chicago area for a twelve-day stand at the Coco Loco Supper Club in south suburban Alsip.

"Be sure to come to see me, Bob," Dick said. "I'd love to get together to talk about the old days."

Returning from the show, I was floating on a cloud. While I wasn't quite sure what would happen when, and if, Dick and I got together again, I knew that I would welcome the chance to renew my acquaintance with the maestro.

CHAPTER TWENTY-ONE

COACH BOVE

A few months later, when Dick returned to the Chicago area to play the Condesa del Mar, I immediately made reservations for Dick's show.

Picking up where we'd left off, Dick and I found how very much we enjoyed each other's company .

Dick was great. A regular guy. In the neighborhood, you know, friends can sit together for hours and talk about all kinds of things — something that we affectionately call 'shooting the bull' — and Dick and I would do just that."

Near the end of Dick's engagement, I was approached by Joan Sodoma, a member of Dick's original fan club, who asked Connie and me to attend a party at a the home of a club member. Feeling like an intruder, I declined the offer but, at Dick's urging, I finally decided to tag along.

Talking over snacks and drinks and making new friends at the party, I got an up-close look at the rapport that Dick had established with his fans. After performing two shows, giving his all to make sure that the audience had had a wonderful time, Dick entertained special requests.

I couldn't get over it! Here was an entertainer who was so appreciative of his fans that he would perform for them with no questions asked.

Continuing to talk with some of the people at the party, I learned that Dick's impromptu performance was not a unique event.

"Dick does this all of the time." a fan club member said. "Whenever we have a party to celebrate the end of an engagement, he performs just like he did this evening."

"It makes you feel special when someone you admire so much returns the admiration in such a nice and sincere way."

Leaving the party, I told my wife, Connie, that Dick was indeed a special person and I vowed to help him in any way I could.

••••••••••

During the mid-seventies, Dick contacted me whenever he was appearing in the Chicago area. He was to appear at Leo Held's renowned "Brown Bear Restaurant" on Chicago's famous Clark Street. I offered to meet Dick at O'Hare International Airport and to drive him to the Brown Bear.

I asked Dick where he'd be staying while performing at the restaurant. He replied that he'd made arrangements to stay at The Continental Hotel on Chicago's famed Michigan Avenue.

It might have seemed a bit presumptuous, but I asked Dick if he'd consider staying with my family for the weekend.

Although touched by his new friend's offer, Dick was unsure of what to do.

"I was afraid that I'd be putting you and your family to a great deal of trouble," Dick recalls. "But when you assured me that that wouldn't be the case, I gratefully accepted."

After Dick's first evening at the restaurant, he spent the night at my home in South Chicago Heights.

The performances at the restaurant were a great success. Each show drew a large and appreciative audience.

In addition to enthralling the Chicago audiences, Dick's performances at the restaurant earned him a new and ardent admirer.

Dick and daughter, Mary, performing at the Brown Bear Restaurant in Chicago, Illinois

Held's mother, Thea, took a special liking to Dick. She attended each performance.

A short time after the successful engagement at The Brown Bear, Dick found that he was once again a popular booking in the Chicago area.

A few weeks later, my family and I drove to O'Hare Field to meet Dick, Leigh, and their daughter, Mary. After her recent success in the Miss USA Pageant, Mary was going to appear with her father on a three-week tour and Leigh, after a brief stop in Chicago, would return to Las Vegas.

Connie, the kids and I were among the many fans awaiting Dick's arrival. As the family walked from the plane, cheers arose from the welcoming throng.

This was the first time that I'd had the chance to meet Leigh and Mary. I couldn't believe the resemblance between mother and daughter. They were both beautiful, sweet women.

Booked for a return engagement at The Brown Bear, Dick and Mary had a successful series of shows. From there, with me acting as driver, they traveled to the Bridge-Vu Theatre in Valparaiso, Indiana for a weekend stint.

After the Indiana engagement, it was back to Illinois for a series of performances at Scottie's Restaurant in Joliet.

"The shows went really well," Dick remembers, "and they were all the more special to me because of Mary appearing with me. She sang beautifully and, each time she appeared, I saw her mother in her."

Planning the rest of his Midwest tour, Dick told me that he would rent a car to travel to shows in Wisconsin, Ohio and Michigan. I suggested that Dick might want to use my car to travel to the shows.

"I just bought this '77 Thunderbird," I told Dick, "and, if it'll save you a few dollars, why not use it?"

Dick was amazed at the kindness of my offer. At first he refused, not wanting to inconvenience our family. Finally he agreed to use the Ford.

The tour would conclude in Flint, Michigan. Afterwards, my family and I traveled to Flint to catch the performance and to pick up the car.

As he left, Dick thanked me, telling me how much he appreciated my generosity. He paid for our motel room in Flint.

Flying back home, Dick felt content about the friendship that had been renewed after so long a time. At last someone from the old days had come to care.

CHAPTER TWENTY-TWO
THE BROWN BEAR

Several months later, Dick called me to say that he would be performing once more at The Brown Bear Restaurant. As had happened before, I met Dick at the airport and drove him to the show. During the weekend engagement, Dick once again stayed at my house.

The shows were a great success, drawing huge crowds of appreciative fans. Dick was thrilled with the reviews and even more so with the filled houses.

Driving to Sunday's show, which was the last of the scheduled performances, I asked Dick if he had talked to Leo Held about a return engagement for the following weekend.

"Bob, that's really nice of you but things like that just don't happen — it's unheard of."

I refused, however, to be put off. That evening, as Dick was performing, I discussed this idea with the restaurant's owner.

"Bob," Held said, "that's a good idea, but I don't know ..."

Held agreed with me that Dick had been drawing good crowds for his shows and that, in turn, the crowds helped the restaurant's business.

"Let's run the idea past my mother, Bob," Held said. "If she okays it, we'll do it."

Racing from the office, I found Mother Held and explained the idea to her. She had grown quite fond of Dick and wholeheartedly supported the idea.

After the show, as Dick was dressing, I told Dick that Leo and Thea wanted to see him in the restaurant's office.

Dick asked what they wanted.

"Come on," I replied, "go find out."

Dick was surprised at being asked to return the following weekend. When he left the office, he had a cat-like grin on his handsome face.

"Bob!" he said pointing at me. "You pulled it off. I forgot that we had talked about my coming back. How'd you do it?"

I repeated the conversations I'd had with Leo and Mama Held and told Dick that they knew a good thing when they had one.

"Come on," Dick told his friend, "I want to go home to call Leigh with the good news."

Thrilled at her husband's good fortune, she asked to speak with Bob. She was so grateful. She couldn't thank me enough and blessed me and my family.

Dick flew to Las Vegas to spend a few days at home before coming back to Chicago for the return engagement.

The shows went extremely well. Dick drew excellent crowds, and the audience, as well as the Held's, were very happy with the performances

Backing up Dick at the shows was Paul Ilgen, the regular pianist at The Brown Bear Restaurant. Ilgen, who had studied classical music while a young man in Germany, impressed Dick with his talent. If Dick had lined up enough bookings, he would have asked Ilgen to go on the road with him as his pianist/conductor. Dick never forgot the pianist's ability.

The happy times experienced at The Brown Bear would soon end, however, as both Leo and Thea Held passed away within a few months of each other in late 1976.

"Through the couple's generosity, and Bob's hard work, I was provided with an opportunity to get on my feet once again," Dick recalls. "I'll never forget those wonderful times."

CHAPTER TWENTY-THREE
FESTA!

In the late seventies, a gentleman from Milwaukee by the name of Paul Iannelli had come up with an idea for a festival to celebrate the Italian way of life.

Forming a group to put together the festival, Iannelli faced difficulties with many members of the Italian community. These people believed that such an idea was a frivolous one and that an Italian Festival would be a waste of time and, worse, would lose money and make the Italian community the laughing-stock of Milwaukee.

Iannelli stood firm. He believed that Italians would support such a venture. He bet that, with the right types of food and entertainment, and with the right location — somewhere near the city's lakefront — the event would be a great success.

Iannelli said that he wanted to keep the festival in Milwaukee's Third Ward, because of its being the original home to many immigrants of Italian heritage. Although the area had been razed for the construction of a new expressway and other so-called improvements, he truly believed that this festival — this monument to the dreams and the way of life of the Italian people — would be a success."

The first Festa was held in 1978, was a great success. With wonderful Italian foods (lasagna, pasta, pizza fritte, beef and sausage sandwiches, fried cauliflower and zucchini, pastries, etc.), games, drinks, and rides, and with entertainers such as singers Johnny Desmond and Johnny Vannelli, the fest drew large and enthusiastic crowds of all ethnic groups.

Building on that initial success, the committee decided to make the Festa a yearly event. As the years passed, the size and scope of the Festa increased until, today, it has become the largest ethnic event in the world.

It was while preparing for the second fest, that Iannelli, who was in the midst of deciding which entertainers to book for the event, heard about Dick Contino's availability.

"I was told that Dick would be a natural for an event such as ours," Iannelli remembers. "Comedian Pat Cooper told me that I'd be missing the boat, if I didn't get Dick to appear on the program."

Acting on Cooper's suggestion, Iannelli contacted Dick to ask if he'd be interested in appearing at the fest.

"I was thrilled when Paul contacted me," Dick said. "I had a gut feeling that, if things worked out well at the fest, it might turn out to be the kick-start that my career needed."

Contino was right.

Dick agreed to appear at the Festa, which would headline Johnny Desmond. Dick telephoned me with the happy news. Driving to Milwaukee, I met Iannelli and off we went to greet Dick at the airport.

As Dick walked from the plane, he embraced me warmly and, turning to Iannelli, extended his hand in greeting.

"Hi! I'm Dick Contino."

From that moment, a bond of friendship existed between the two men, a bond that would, indeed, kick-start Contino's comeback.

Playing to large and enthusiastic throngs of fans from all across the midwestern United States, Dick was a huge success at the fest. He was in his element — these were his people, the kinds of people that he had grown up with. He felt comfortable with them and that comfort was apparent in everything he did."

"I had a great time at the fest," Dick remembers. "One of my most cherished memories is of walking through the festival grounds and of meeting the people. They were so friendly and so encouraging, never pushy — it was a wonderful time."

Dick and I looked forward to the next year's Festa. When I learned that the fest wouldn't be inviting Dick back to entertain the following year, I called Iannelli to ask the reason.

"Bob," Iannelli said, "Dick was great and he drew wonderful crowds but, because it's a new event, we feel that we need to change the entertainers each year."

I would not be deterred, however, and told Paul that Dick should be the mainstay at the festival. I was sure that he would draw good crowds and that he would put on a wonderful show.

Another thing I realized was that Dick would bring a loyalty to the fest that was too often missing from many entertainers.

I knew Dick would do well at the fest and that he would show his gratitude by appearing each year, no matter what.

Iannelli, being sympathetic to my words and to the financial difficulties facing Dick, agreed to try to get him booked for a repeat performance.

"I can't promise anything, Bob," he said, "I have to present the idea to the committee, but I'll try my best."

Several days later, Iannelli called me with the good news that the committee had agreed to book Dick for a second year.

Justifying the faith that his friends had in him, Dick made a triumphant return to the fest. The crowds that he drew exceeded the ones from the preceding year and, with each show, the word spread like wild-fire that Dick Contino was

Dick at one of his performances

"knocking them dead" at the Pabst Stage.

Because of the outstanding success of Dick's shows at the festival, two months later Dick was booked to headline the annual fund-raiser for the Italian Community Center.

Dick put on a wonderful program at the Performing Arts Theatre. The place was packed. Over two thousand people attended the fund-raiser and, believe me, Dick was in his element.

Many of the people in attendance that evening were members of Dick's original Milwaukee fan club. It made Dick feel good to see so many of the fans who had come to see him perform years ago at the city's Riverside Theatre.

The fund-raiser headlined by Dick was a tremendous success, allowing the Community Center to continue its support of many programs throughout the Milwaukee area.

The Italian-American entertainer and the hard-hat city began a love affair. During the ensuing years Dick would work closely with the people of the festival committee, appearing at promotional events and other activities whenever asked to do so.

Once Dick called me at my hotel to ask if I'd accompany him to the fairgrounds at about noon. A man who was dying of cancer desperately wanted to meet Dick Contino. He was being brought from the local hospital for the festival.

Of course, I went with Dick to meet the man. We waited for two hours before learning that the man had been delayed at the hospital. His doctors were concerned about the effect of the trip. They wondered if the strain would be too much. Dick offered to travel to the hospital to meet the fan but was told that, in addition to meeting him, the gentleman wanted to see him perform.

Finally, the doctors relented. The man was brought to the

fairgrounds in a wheelchair. Dick sat with the dying man, chatting about music and mutual interests. When it came time for Dick to perform, Dick made sure that the man was placed near the stage and he dedicated the performance to him.

Sometime later, Dick inquired as to the man's condition. "I learned that he had died shortly after the fest," Dick remembers. "I was glad that I had been able to spend that time with him."

•••••••••

It was while performing at his sixth fest that Dick would add another chapter to his expanding legend. While waiting to go on stage, Paul had invited Dick to view the fireworks that closed each evening's fest. Enthralled by such displays since his childhood, Dick watched in amazement as the lights radiated a brilliant and colorful display above the choppy waters of Lake Michigan.

While viewing the display, he mentioned to Paul that he'd like to meet "the bomb squad" — the men who created such a remarkable show.

Iannelli introduced Dick the entertainer to Sam Bartollotta and his crew. Bartollotta explained to Dick that his family had been in the business for years and that he and his crew, including his son, John, traveled across the country providing countless festivals and celebrations with the colorful displays.

After a lengthy conversation had established a mutual admiration society between Dick and the men, Bartollotta invited the entertainer to join them the following day in setting the fireworks and igniting the display.

"I was thrilled!" Dick remembers, "I was like a kid on his birthday. I thought that being a part of the fireworks' team would be the neatest thing in the world."

While learning of the subtleties of the fireworks craft, Dick began to think about incorporating the massive display into his program. He decide to close his medley, "The American Trilogy," by finishing with an explosive rendition of the immortal "Battle Hymn of the Republic." This would provide the perfect opportunity for melding the stirring music with the awe-inspiring fireworks show.

His keyboardist, Corky Bennett, and Dick discussed how they could work out the split second timing that was needed to ensure the desired effect of coordinating the explosions with the proper musical accompaniment."

After a while, Dick, Bennett and the crew decided that the only way to pull off the event was by using a walkie-talkie. Bennett, on-stage at the Festa, would signal Bartollotta who was stationed nearly a mile away from the entertainment area, five seconds before the explosions were needed. The expert "bomb squad" would do the rest.

"I was excited about the event," Dick remembers, "knowing that, if it could be done, we would provide the festa-goers with a once-in-a-lifetime entertainment thrill."

"Of course, we never had the luxury of rehearsing the number so you can bet that I said lots of Hail Mary's that day."

That afternoon, as Dick launched into his finale, everyone who knew of the plans waited with baited breath.

I was standing backstage, nervous as a cat. I was, literally, holding my breath to see what would happen."

To the surprise of the crew, Dick seemed extraordinarily confident about the success of the venture.

"Hey, the festival had been my good luck piece — I knew that everything'd be okay."

"Okay" was an understatement.

Bennett radioed Bartollotta and, at the very moment that Dick launched into the "Hymn's" refrain, the sky came alive with a series of brilliant and colorful flashes and explosions that underscored the stirring notes.

The people went wild — they stood as one, watching with open mouths as the performance went off like clockwork.

When Dick left the stage, the audience roared its approval.

"I got goose bumps," Dick remembers. "To know that I affected people in such a way was a very humbling experience."

The next day, Dick made certain that all of the members of Bartolotta's crew were recognized for their important role in the success of the finale by bringing them onto the stage for a bow.

When questioned as to why he had taken the time to introduce the men of the "bomb squad," Dick quietly replied, "I had to — they were as important to the success of yesterday's show as I had been."

••••••••••

As a result of his success at the fest, Dick received a memorable booking. A chieftain of a branch of the notorious Chicago "mob" requested that Dick entertain for his daughter's wedding.

"After agreeing to appear at the wedding," Dick recalls, "I was told that I would be contacted with the necessary information concerning the event."

On the day of the wedding, Dick flew into Chicago.

I met Dick at the airport and we drove to a designated location in Maywood, Illinois, where we were met by the longest, shiniest limousine that you could imagine.

Parking the car, we walked to the waiting limo. The driver opened the rear door and motioned for us to get in.

Dick waved to someone waiting in a parked car. This gesture aroused the curiosity of the chauffeur.

"Whoa," he told Dick, "who're you waving to?"

Realizing that he might have overstepped his bounds, Dick hastily explained to the driver that the man in the car was Mike Roeder, the drummer that Dick used for all of his Midwestern appearances.

"Can he ride with us?" Dick asked, sheepishly.

The driver shook his head.

"My orders were to come to this location and to pick up you and Mr. Bove. No one else gets in the car."

Realizing the futility of arguing, Dick asked what they would do with Roeder.

"He'll just have to follow us," the driver shrugged.

Roeder obediently fell in behind the limo.

"Hey," I asked the driver, "will my car be okay here?"

The man looked at me with what could be termed amusement in his eye.

"Your car?" he asked. "Oh, yeah, your car will be fine. We guarantee it."

I shrugged, looked at Dick, and nodded.

Arriving at the wedding, we were ushered into a room and told to rest comfortably until someone would come for them.

A half-hour later, a tall, dark, muscular man dressed in a beautifully-tailored tuxedo, entered the room. Expecting to be led to the dining room, Dick, Roeder and I scrambled to our feet.

Suddenly, the man stopped. Turning a cold eye toward me and Roeder, he pointed.

"You and you, have a seat. Mr. F_____ wants to see Mr. Contino."

With a look of uncertainty on his face, Dick left the room.

In his absence, we spotted an open bottle of champagne. Looking at each other, we shrugged our shoulders and reached for the magnum.

We spent a very happy half-hour in that room.

At last, we were taken to meet our host. Graciously refusing the man's offer of food, although famished, we decided to sup on the fabulous desserts that had been prepared the event. Following our host into a room next to the dining area — a room that was filled, as far as the eye could see, with a variety of the finest examples of the Italian baker's art.

Mr. F_____ handed each of us a plate and, taking me by the hand, began to pile desserts on the dish. Dick doesn't eat sweets but, what could he do, he didn't want to offend the man. I glanced at him and gave him a wink. He went along for the ride.

Knowing that my friend wouldn't be able to digest the sweet treats, I whispered to Dick that I would assist him in his time of need.

"I'll take just one or two things," I told him, "and I'll help you eat what's on your plate."

Relieved at his friend's plan, Dick carried on.

The performance that evening was a great success. The radiant bride, thrilled at the "surprise guest," embraced her father, thanking him for the special show. Dick, backed by Roeder and a ten-piece orchestra, played for over an hour, performing a set that he had used while playing the finest clubs in the country.

"That was some night," Dick recalls. "I'll tell you, I've been to lots of places and seen lots of things, but I never — ever —

saw furs and jewelry like I saw at that wedding."

"If somebody'd made a score that night, well he'd have been set for life. Of course, his life would have probably been a very short one."

Following the show, Dick and his friends returned to the dressing room where, after a while, an emissary of Mr. F_____ stopped by to pay Dick for his performance and to compliment him on the outstanding show.

After changing our clothes, Dick and I piled into the limo. Roeder followed closely behind. We were driven to where our car was parked.

On our way to my house, we spent the time discussing the day's events. It was, we agreed, a most unusual and exciting experience.

CHAPTER TWENTY-FOUR

ENTERTAINMENT UNLIMITED

Several months later. Dick was again booked into the Chicago area. As always, I was there to meet him at the airport.

As we were driving to my house, I mentioned that I'd heard Ray Charles' version of "America" on the radio. I asked Dick if he might be able to work the song into his act as a patriotic number.

"You know, Bob," Dick answered, "you might have an idea there. I've heard the song and I agree that it's a fine arrangement. Let me think about it."

Nothing came of my suggestion at that series of performances but, a few months later, when Dick returned to the Festa Italiana in Milwaukee, I was to see how well my idea would work.

I was standing backstage at Dick's opening performance as he began to play "The American Trilogy. As he segued into the "Battle Hymn," he looked my way and flashed me a smile."

A few moments later, Dick began to play "America." The effect on the audience was electrifying.

He continued to play. The audience stood up and, swayed in time to the music, singing and humming along.

At the conclusion of the show, the audience roared its approval at the performance and many cried for a reprise of "The Trilogy."

Walking offstage, Dick handed me his Petosa and patted me on the shoulder.

"Dick, you son-of-a-gun! That was really great. I thought that you'd forgotten about my suggestion."

"Bob," the entertainer smiled, "how could I forget my friend's advice? Just don't go looking for any royalties, though."

"You never cease to amaze me," I said.

••••••••••

Impressed by the continued success of the festa in Milwaukee, Anthony Fornelli, a prominent Chicago attorney associated with the Italian organization UNICO, wanted to create an Italian Festival on Chicago's Navy Pier. Fornelli contacted Paul Iannelli and asked for his help in getting the event off the ground.

"Anthony asked me many questions," Iannelli remembers, "and was particularly interested in how to go about securing the best entertainment for the fest."

At Iannelli's urging, Fornelli contacted Dick who agreed to headline the inaugural event. Also appearing at the festival would be Dick's friend, singer Anna Maria Alberghetti.

This time, instead of staying with our family, Dick would spend the three days of the festival housed in a hotel on Chicago's famous Lake Shore Drive.

Arriving for his rehearsal on the opening day of the fest, Dick walked with Fornelli and me to the area where he would be performing. Three stages had been erected for the fest and, as the event's headliner, Dick assumed that he would be performing on center stage. To his surprise, Fornelli walked past the middle stage and led Dick to the stage at the far end of the pier.

"Hey, Tony," Dick asked, "What's going on? I'm headlining this show and you got me down here in the boondocks."

"Dick," he said, "you're performing at the end of the pier because of the crowds that you're going to attract."

"What's that?"

"Look, Dick, the pier is too narrow to put you on the middle stage because all of the people who'll come to see you will block others from reaching the far stage. Believe me, we're not slighting you - this is the best stage."

Unfazed by the man's plea, Dick grumbled his disapproval and threatened to cancel his appearance and return home.

Fornelli's eyes pleaded with me to do something with my friend.

"Dick, Dick, calm down," I urged him. "You heard what Tony told you and, believe me, he's right. I've been here before and the pier's too narrow to hold the crowds you'll attract."

After a while, Dick saw the logic and the show went on as scheduled. Drawing large and enthusiastic throngs, Dick's performance was the hit of the opening night. After seeing that Fornelli's words were true, Dick called the man aside and apologized for the childish display that had occurred earlier that day.

"I'm sorry, Tony," Dick said, "but I have a terrible time accepting rejection. When you brought me down to the end stage, I thought that I'd done something wrong — that you changed your mind about my being your headliner.

Fornelli grasped his hand.

"Dick," he said, "think nothing of it. You were wonderful tonight."

Preparing to leave Chicago after his successful performances at the fest, Dick again went to see Fornelli.

"Tony," the entertainer said, "I had a wonderful time at the festival and I wanted to stop by to tell you how much I appreciate all that you've done for me."

"It was my pleasure, Dick," he answered. "Everything went so well that, if the committee approves the idea, I'd like to have you back next year."

Dick thanked the man and, with me at his side, left for the hotel.

"You know, Bob," Dick told me as we drove to O'Hare Field on the following morning, "I've got a good feeling about the people that I've met while doing these fests. Paul Iannelli and Tony Fornelli seem like really great people — the kind of people that you like to associate yourself with."

"Dick," I replied, "these men are like family. They care about people. They care about you."

Dick rested his head against the seat. In no time, he fell asleep, relaxed by the hum of the car's engine.

••••••••••

One year later, Dick was booked for a triumphant return to Chicago's Italian Festa. Again, crowds in record numbers swarmed to see the legendary performer.

While appearing at the fest, Dick met with Paul Iannelli who had traveled from Milwaukee to enjoy the event. While talking to his mentor from Wisconsin, Dick learned that, on the following day, the Italian Community Center of Milwaukee would be conducting a celebrity dinner. The dinner was the culminating event of its annual "Italian Open," a golf outing featuring famous Italian-American sports figures.

"I was wondering, Dick," Iannelli asked, "if there's any

chance that you might be able to perform at the dinner."

Although scheduled to perform at the Festa on that Sunday afternoon, Dick agreed to appear at the banquet that evening.

At the dinner, Dick dined with Paul Iannelli and his family, surrounded by such athletic luminaries as Willie Mosconi, billiard champion, and Carmen Basilio, welterweight champion, Ron Luciano, American League baseball umpire, and Nat Rosasco, founder and President of Northwestern Golf Company. Enjoying the pleasure of their company, Dick spent an enjoyable couple of hours listening to stories of their athletic accomplishments.

"Carmen Basilio was a particular favorite of mine," Dick recalls. "As we talked, I mentioned to him that my mother's brother, Ralph Giordano, had fought as Young Corbett III and had been Welterweight Champion of the World in the early 1930's. It pleased me that Carmen remembered my uncle.

At the appointed time, Dick went on stage to a thunderous round of applause. For well over an hour, the entertainer held the capacity crowd in the palm of his hand as he performed all of the numbers for which he had become famous.

As the show ended, the audience rose as one to give Dick a well-deserved standing ovation.

"Dick! Dick!" a voice called.

Nat Rosasco was motioning for him to come to his side.

"Dick, I just remembered!" Rosasco said. "You told me that you love to play golf and my company is coming out with a brand-new line of equipment. It's called—don't laugh now—the "metal wood" - you know, drivers and fairway woods made of steel instead of persimmon or maple."

Dick mentioned that he'd heard about the new technology.

"The next time that you're in Chicago, come over to the factory and I'll see that you're measured for a set!"

Thrilled at the offer, he thanked Rosasco but, thinking that the gift was too generous, declined.

"Dick," Rosasco laughed, "don't worry about it. Hell, I own the company."

The two men laughed and, a few weeks later, Dick was in Chicago picking up his set of custom-made golf clubs.

CHAPTER TWENTY-FIVE
BACK TO CHI-TOWN

The decade of the Eighties dawned with Dick's career on an upward note based, primarily, on his success at the growing number of ethnic fests. Still, he hungered for recognition on a more expansive basis. Once again, that friends came to his aid.

One day while talking to Dick about a performance he had just finished in Florida, I casually asked if he'd consider giving a concert in my home town of Chicago Heights.

At first, unsure of the viability of such an effort, he begged off.

"Bob," he said, "I'd love to perform in concert in Chicago Heights but, you know, I'm not exactly a household name any more."

He went on to tell his friend that successful concerts are built around "hot" entertainers — people whose names are immediately recognizable.

I let the matter drop, realizing that Dick was uncomfortable with the idea.

The next day my phone rang and, to my surprise, it was Leigh Contino on the line.

"Bob" she began, "Dick was mentioning me about your idea for concerts in Chicago Heights. Tell me more about it, please."

I explained to Leigh that my plan was to involve the members of the fan club in the promotion of the event and that the concerts would be presented at Bloom High School's

Workman Auditorium on Saturday and Sunday evenings. I added that arrangements could be made with local restaurateurs to have Dick meet with his fans at their establishments before and/or after each show.

Thrilled at my ideas, Leigh told me to go ahead with the plans for the concerts.

"Leigh," I said, apprehensively, "Dick wasn't excited about the idea ...."

Leigh cut in.

"Bob, just go ahead with the plans. Trust me, I'll get him enthused about the concerts."

Acting on Leigh's suggestion, I arranged a meeting with the officers of Dick's fan club. Gathering at my house, I informed the members of my plans. I solicited their help in promoting and financing the event.

I was pleased with the response of the members. They were determined to support the concert although, as it should be, some members were concerned about the cost of promoting such a venture and wondered about ways of ensuring its success.

I explained that I would get an estimate as to how much it would cost to produce the show. I also promised to secure legal advice pertaining to matters such as liability insurance, and that I would notify them of my findings.

A week later, I informed the club that the concerts could be produced at a nominal cost. The members would be responsible for the cost of the liability insurance in addition to the cost of printing tickets and promotional material for the event. If each member would donate twenty-five dollars to cover the initial cost of promoting the concert, everything would be covered. Any additional expenses would be paid through revenue generated by ticket sales.

BACK TO CHI-TOWN

About one week after their initial conversation, Dick called me to confirm his participation in the event.

"Dick, you sure?" I asked.

"Hey, Bob," Dick answered, "I'm sure. What can I tell you — Leigh wants me to do it and, whatever Leigh wants, Leigh gets."

Nevertheless, Dick was still unsure as to how a concert would go over. He admitted his fear that the event would be a failure and stated again that he didn't want us to be saddled with a losing proposition.

It was then that I told Dick of the interest that such a concert would generate.

"Dick, things will turn out great. Listen, I called about two hundred people and asked what they thought of your appearing in town. Believe me when I tell you that almost everybody said that they'd love to see you."

"Heck," I continued, "there's people I talked to who remember seeing you at the Lincoln-Dixie Theatre in 1948. They still talk about the show you put on that day."

Buoyed by the news he'd heard, Dick became excited about the prospect.

"Go for it, Bob."

••••••••••

The next three months would be filled with activity. First, we secured as background musicians the performers who had worked with Dick at a previous engagement at The Blue Max nightclub in Rosemont's Hyatt Regency Hotel. Then we had to get the promotional material distributed. Next, we had to arrange for the dispersal of tickets. Finally, we coordinated the dates for the concert. I was a very busy man.

The concerts were scheduled for Saturday and Sunday, June 7 and 8, 1980. I arranged to meet with members of the fan club at The Brown Bear Restaurant in early March when Dick would be appearing there. At that meeting, members would receive tickets to be sold for the concerts.

As May approached, tickets for the event were selling at a rapid pace. The success of the advance sale provided me with a wonderful idea.

I called Dick in Las Vegas and told him how well tickets were selling. I asked if he'd be interested in bringing his entire family to the shows.

Amazed at the suggestion, Dick asked, "Bob, can you afford to pay for my family, too? Bringing Leigh, my mom and the kids to Chicago — we're talking big money.".

I assured Dick that the money to cover such expenses was already in the bank, and that everything would work out just fine.

Dick, grateful for my courteous suggestion, told me to plan on his family's attending the event.

"We'll look forward to seeing you on June 6."

••••••••••

Arriving at the airport on Friday afternoon, Dick, Leigh, Mama Contino, and the children were welcomed by my family, myself and members of the original fan club. Piling into the limo that had been secured for the trip, Dick and the family were driven to their hotel in Chicago Heights.

After resting a few hours, the Contino clan met with fans for dinner at Savoia's, a restaurant at which Dick had dined following his 1948 performance at the Lincoln-Dixie Theatre.

After the meal, the Bamonti's, the owners of the restaurant, joined Dick and his family, regaling them with stories. Thoroughly enjoying themselves, Dick, Leigh, Mama, and the children had a wonderful evening.

The next afternoon, June 7, 1980, I went to the hotel to pick up Dick for his rehearsal. When he arrived at the auditorium, Dick was amazed at the beauty of the high school facility.

"I was astounded that such a magnificent facility could be found in a high school," Dick said. "The setting, the acoustics, everything was first class."

Renewing his friendship with the musicians who would back him up, Dick ran through the numbers that would form the basis for the evening's concert.

Following the rehearsal, Dick and I discussed the evening's show over a light lunch. I assured the entertainer that everything would work out fine and, after some additional conversation, Dick returned to his hotel to rest.

••••••••••

Doors for the 8:00 p.m. performance opened one hour before show time. A steady stream of fans made its way into the auditorium. The enthusiasm of the people attending the show made it apparent that the evening would be a success.

As a surprise for Dick, I arranged for Paul Iannelli and Henry Piano (one of Iannelli's co-horts in organizing the Milwaukee fest) to attend the show. Piano, in fact, had agreed to act as Master of Ceremonies for the program.

Backstage, Dick, ever anxious, awaited the start of the concert like a fighter awaiting the opening bell of a championship fight. His family was seated in the front row of the auditorium, surrounded by Dick's cheering fans.

At the appointed time, the lights dimmed and the near-capacity crowd grew silent. Henry Piano walked onto the stage, microphone in hand.

"Ladies and gentlemen," he intoned, "it is my honor to introduce to you a man who's a legend in show business — a man who, through his outstanding musical performances, has been instrumental in securing the success of the Italian Fest in Milwaukee — a man who has earned a special place in the hearts of fans all around the world — here he is, 'the Valentino of the Accordion,' DICK CONTINO!!!"

Dick walked onto the stage with an assured air. It was plain to see that the crowd would be treated to a memorable experience. Interspersing friendly chatter with the songs that the fans had come to hear, Dick cast a spell which transported the members of the audience to magical heights. He performed songs with an international flavor — "La Tarantella," "Mama" and "Malaguena." He performed several medleys including such standards as "Exodus," "Hava Nagila," and "Sunrise, Sunset," and reprised such hits as "Tico Tico," "Sabre Dance," and, his signature song, "Lady of Spain." The audience roared when he impersonated Dean Martin's singing of "Everybody Loves Somebody." They heartily applauded his versatility following his piano rendition of "Flight of the Bumble Bee."

Having performed for over an hour, Dick asked if the audience would like an intermission.

"NO!" the fans roared. "Keep playing!"

Smiling, the performer acknowledged their response by breaking into a stirring rendition of "Granada," which elicited a thunderous response from the packed house.

Pausing at the end of the number, Dick took the opportunity to introduce his family. His daughter, Mary, urged on by her adoring father, walked on-stage and entertained the crowd by singing the Nat King Cole classic, "Love." Next, Leigh joined her husband for a medley of songs, closing with "You Made Me Love You," a song that had assumed a special place in the couple's life since they had heard it while honeymooning in Hawaii. It had become "their song." The crowd went wild.

At the close of the two-hour concert — concert being a poor word choice since the audience, enthralled by the entertainer, had made it more of a love-fest — Dick left the stage to wild applause.

Accompanied by my wife, I went backstage to congratulate Dick on his performance. Spotting Dick giving Leigh a quick kiss, I said, "Hey, can't that wait 'til later?"

Laughing, Dick grabbed my hand.

"Bob, thank you, thank you a million times for all that you've done," he said. "I can't tell you how much tonight meant to me."

Amplifying her husband's words, Leigh hugged me.

"Think nothing of it," I told them. "Helping friends is what life's all about."

"Don't forget," he added, "we've got another show tomorrow."

Dick nodded.

"Come on, let's get some pizza," I suggested. "We've got people waiting to see you."

At the close of the concert, I had announced to the audience that a party in honor of Dick would be held at Aurelio's Pizza Parlor and that everyone in the audience was welcome to stop by to say hello to Dick and Leigh. Over one hundred fans took advantage of the opportunity.

After enjoying Aurelio's famed deep-dish pizza, Dick and his family toured the restaurant, thanking Joe Aurelio for his gracious hospitality. Dick mentioned to Leigh that he hadn't been treated so well in many, many years.

Returning to the dinner table, Dick called me to his side.

"Bob," he said, "do me a favor. Go out to the car and get my accordion — I feel like playing."

Although surprised at the request, I did as he asked.

Strapping on his accordion, Dick strolled through the restaurant performing for the appreciative audience.

"It was like the old days," Dick recalls, "when I would play all night long for my family and friends in Fresno."

Fielding requests from his fans, Dick played all of the tunes the people wanted to hear. It was, in many ways, a night that would live forever in Dick's heart.

Seeing the rapport that Dick established with the audience, Aurelio hit upon the idea of opening a restaurant on the West Coast or in Hawaii, wherever Dick and Leigh wanted, where Dick would be the "house entertainer" in addition to being a partner. Joe proposed that the restaurant could serve as a venue for displaying the talents of the entire Contino family.

"When you're home, Dick, you perform," Aurelio said. "When you're on tour, Mary and Leigh can entertain."

"Think about it," the restaurateur urged.

Dick liked the idea.

"I will," he promised.

••••••••••

The Sunday performance on June 8 mirrored the one that had preceded it. Dick gave the crowd everything that it wanted, providing his fans with a show the like of which they'd never seen.

Late that evening, while driving Dick and his family back to their hotel, I told the entertainer that I'd pick him up in the morning to go to the bank to close out the account that I'd opened in his name. I told him I'd see him about eight o'clock.

The next morning, right on time, I arrived to take Dick to the bank. On the way, the men discussed the concerts.

"Bob," Dick asked, "I know that we had good crowds for both shows, but I also know that we had expenses that ate into the profits. How do you think we did?"

I shrugged.

"If my records are right, Dick," I said, "you should clear about $5,500."

Dick was amazed.

"$5,500 ...... Bob, you sure?"

"I think so, Dick. We'll find out for sure in a few minutes."

Closing out the account, Dick and I listened to the bank teller as she told them that the account contained $6,500.84."

The men exchanged a surprised glance.

"Excuse me, ma'am," I asked, "did you say $6,500?"

The teller nodded in agreement.

"Have I made a mistake?"

Smiling, Dick and I shook our heads.

As the teller closed the account, Dick turned to me and said that he could not believe how successful the shows had been.

"Bob," he said, "I've been entertaining for more than thirty years and this is, by far, the most money that I've ever made for two shows. I can't wait to tell Leigh and the family the good news."

Before returning to Las Vegas, Leigh and Mama Contino sought me out to offer me their heartfelt thanks.

"Bob," Leigh said, "this has been one of the highlights of Dick's entertainment career. And, I'm not ashamed to tell you that the money means a great deal to us — this'll keep us from having to dip into our savings. I know that I'll never forget all that you and the members of his fan club did for us."

Watching Dick and his family board the plane that would take them home to Las Vegas, I had tears in my eyes. Just knowing that I had been associated with an event that had provided them with such happiness gave me immense satisfaction.

CHAPTER TWENTY-SIX
"YOURS"

The popularity of the concerts in Chicago Heights soon provided another opportunity that would assist Dick on his "comeback trail."

Al Waltner, a proprietor of a prominent auction house in Monee, Illinois, called me one afternoon to tell me that he was a great fan of the entertainer. He had requested twenty reserved tickets for Dick's Sunday night concert. Although he would be personally unable to attend the program, Waltner purchased the tickets as gifts for some of his best customers. Waltner told me that he wanted his friends to have the opportunity of seeing Dick in concert. Naturally, I arranged for the tickets to be reserved.

I thought nothing of the occurrence. I assumed that Waltner was just another Dick Contino fan. Imagine, then, my surprise when, a few days after the concerts, he called me to discuss the possibility of Dick's recording an album — an album that Waltner would produce, promote and market.

"Bob," Waltner said, "my phone's been ringing off the hook. People have been calling to tell me how much they enjoyed the program and what a fantastic performer Dick is. After the first couple of calls, I started thinking that maybe Dick should make a record. I think there's a good market for it."

I told Waltner that I couldn't make any promises or negotiate in Dick's name. I did, however, promise to call Dick to let him know of the request.

After several frantic calls, I was finally able to reach Dick. When I discussed Waltner's idea with him, he chuckled at the thought.

"Bob, is he serious? Does this guy have any idea how much money it takes to produce and market an album?"

"Look," Dick continued, "if he wants a recording of my show or of some particular songs, just tell him to come to see me perform and to arrange for the program to be recorded."

I told Dick that the man was, indeed, serious about the request. I promised to let Waltner know of Dick's concerns.

The following day, I met with Waltner and informed the man of my discussion with Dick.

Waltner, while disappointed at Dick's apprehension, asked me to once again approach him with the idea.

"I don't want to record one of Dick's shows," Waltner said, "I really want to do this on a professional level. Please, Bob, try to convince him"

Once again I called Dick. Eventually I got Dick to agree to discuss the matter with Waltner.

Dick was on his way to a performance in south Florida. He gave me the telephone number of the hotel where he'd be staying and told me that, if Waltner were really serious about the recording, he should contact him there."

Encouraged at the prospect of working with his favorite entertainer, Waltner contacted Dick and convinced him to record the album.

Right after speaking with Dick, Waltner called me. He couldn't thank me enough for the role that I'd played in arranging the project.

The entrepreneur hoped to record the album in early 1981. Working with his daughter and partner Linda, he formed the

Mercedes McGee Record Company through which the album would be distributed. In an effort to secure the finest recording studio, producer, and musicians, Waltner contacted Gary Loizzo, former lead singer of the pop band, The American Breed, who had retired from show business to become a record producer. Loizzo had opened Pumpkin Studios in Oak Lawn, Illinois and was working with, among others, the wildly successful rock group, Styx. After brief negotiations, the recording session was scheduled for February.

Given complete artistic control of the project, Dick decided to use, among others, his old friends Mike Roeder, Warren Kime and Paul Ilgen to front the studio musicians that would accompany him on the recording. Becoming more enthusiastic with each passing day, Dick even wrote several new arrangements to be included on the disc.

The day before the session was to begin, I picked up Dick at O'Hare Field.

I could tell from the way he acted that Dick was up for the project. After all, this would be his first recording session in nearly twenty years and he was determined to give it his best shot.

Dick told me that, although he'd recorded many albums before, this would be the first time that he had been granted absolute control of every aspect of the album-making process.

"When I recorded for Mercury and the other labels, I was always told what songs to play and given standard arrangements to follow. Now, with the opportunity of selecting the songs that I want to record and having the chance to create the arrangements that I've dreamed of for so many years, well, I want this project to come off really, really well."

Arriving at the studio early in the morning, Dick was introduced to Loizzo. He renewed his friendship with the musicians with whom he would work. Working through the arrangements, Dick carefully charted the progression of each work with the engineer and musicians. His diligence and knowledge greatly impressed Loizzo.

"I thought that I'd be recording just an accordion player," Loizzo said. "I'd never heard of Dick and didn't expect very much. But, I've gotta tell you, when Dick began to play and I saw the intensity, passion and artistic ability that he brought to each number, well, I was blown away."

Al and Linda Waltner, who attended the majority of the recording sessions were also extremely impressed with Dick's genius. With each take, the duo became more and more committed to the project.

Songs covered in the album ranged from standards such as "New York, New York," "Yours," "Lady of Spain," and "Beer Barrel Polka," to a pair of new pieces written by Dick, "What It Is" and "My Kingdom," a number that Dick had intended for Kenny Rogers.

"When we finished the session, I decided to keep "My Kingdom," Dick said. "I figured, what the hell, Kenny'd had enough good songs."

While preparing to record the album's finale, "The Battle Hymn of the Republic," Dick entertained a suggestion from one of the musicians about using background singers for the song's chorus. Although he liked the idea, Dick thought that the expense of hiring the singers for the number would prohibit the possibility of adding the vocal.

"I talked things over with Al and Linda," Dick said, "and they loved the idea. They had no qualms about spending the extra money to secure the product that I wanted."

The producers were so impressed with the singers' performance during "The Battle Hymn," that they discussed with

Dick performing at the Monee Auction - Al Waltner, producer of album "Yours", in the background, 1980

Dick the possibility of using vocals in other numbers. Dick, happy with the suggestion, decided to use the singers on "What It Is," and, of course, "My Kingdom."

When the album was finished, Dick and the Waltners were extremely proud of the record. Deciding that telemarketing would provide the best opportunity for reaching Dick's fans, Waltner contracted with WGN Television to run commercials for the record. For his part, Dick would appear on several television and radio programs to "plug" the product.

A very special moment in the couple's happy marriage occurred while Leigh was accompanying Dick on a promotional tour of his album. During an appearance in Chicago, Dick and Leigh were driving with me when they passed a sign that said I-57 South - Champaign/Memphis.

Leigh was taken aback when she saw the sign.

"Bob," she asked, "are we close to Memphis? Oh, how I wish I could go back there — it's been so long since I've been able to spend time with my old, dear friends."

When I explained to Leigh that Memphis was nearly five hundred miles from Chicago, the actress grew silent and smiled wistfully.

"Oh, well, that's too bad," she sighed. "It would have been a wonderful trip."

Nothing more was said about Leigh's dream trip until later when Dick and I were alone at a restaurant.

"You know, Dick," I said, "you've got some free time before your next commitment. Why don't you take Leigh down to Memphis? I'm sure that Al would loan you a car for the trip. You know that Leigh would love it."

Dick turned to his friend.

"Bob, you're right. That'd be great. For a long time, Leigh's been talking about going home and I know that it'd mean a great deal to her to be able to visit Memphis and Covington once again."

After a quick phone call to Waltner, and a brief discussion, the trip was arranged. For seven days the couple traveled around the south like a pair of love-struck teenagers. They sat and kissed in the moonlight, walked in the rain (something that Leigh loved and missed terribly since they'd moved to the desert), ate romantic dinners, and visited Leigh's childhood friends. When the pair returned to Chicago, they seemed more in love than ever.

Leigh called me one evening to thank me for my role in arranging the trip.

"Thank you, Bob. The trip meant more to me than I can ever say."

Back on the promotion trail, Dick appeared on radio and television programs such as "The Lee Philip Show," "The Clark Weber Show" and "The Warren Freiberg Show." During his appearances on the programs, Dick, after encountering some initial hostility, was able to establish a rapport with the tele-journalists.

"Lee opened the program by asking me about the old problems," Dick recalled ruefully. "To her credit, though, she gave me a chance to explain my side of the situation and then went on to other things. I was very grateful for her professionalism and warmth in handling the show."

The Freiberg show proved a different story.

"Everyone knows of Warren's right-wing, bombastic approach," Dick said, "and I should have been prepared for the bombs that came my way. Well, right off, he tried to put me on the defensive by hammering away at my conviction and taking things to the extreme."

Keeping his famous temper in check, Dick explained to

Freiberg what had happened during the early fifties and then went on to relate his service experiences and what had happened in the years since his discharge.

"I could see by Warren's eyes that he wasn't aware of the fact that I had been in the Army, had served in Korea, and had put up with a great deal of torment in the years since I'd returned home."

Going against his radio persona, Freiberg heard Dick's story and, after listening in silence, apologized to the entertainer for his hostile attitude.

"Dick," Freiberg said, "I never knew that you served your country, were shipped to Korea, or received an honorable discharge. I would like to issue a public apology for the hard time that I've given you and would like to invite you to return to my program to discuss your life and any new ventures you shall pursue."

In a few, short months, Freiberg would make good his invitation and invite Dick to appear on his Chicago-based television show.

And so it went for a period of months. The album, although never breaking onto the charts, became a consistent seller via mail order and wherever Dick performed.

As for Waltner, he was satisfied that he'd had the chance to work with and to become part of the comeback of the legendary Dick Contino.

CHAPTER TWENTY-SEVEN

LEIGH

During the closing months of 1980, Dick had become increasingly concerned about Leigh' health. She hadn't been feeling well and Dick feared that the dreaded cancer had returned.

In early 1981, while Dick was performing in the Chicago area, he received an invitation to make a repeat visit to "The Warren Freiberg Show." While waiting to go on camera, Dick listened with interest as another guest, a physician, talked with Freiberg about several new and radical cancer treatments.

"When I heard the doctor talk about the possibilities of arresting cancer through proper nutrition, I thought immediately of Leigh," Dick said. "Believe me, I hung on every word."

Talking with the doctor after the program, Dick explained Leigh's problems and asked if any physician near Las Vegas might be able to help Leigh with these new treatments. Given the name of a doctor in St. George, Utah, Dick couldn't wait to tell Leigh about what he'd learned.

"We made the trip to Utah and learned from the doctor of the feasibility of the new treatment," Dick recalled. "After conducting a series of tests, he prescribed a special diet that, we hoped, would help stop the spread of the cancer."

Although Leigh followed the prescribed treatment for several months, the hoped-for cure did not take place. While she did her best to keep up a good front for her family, Leigh knew that she was growing weaker and weaker.

In September of 1981, the members of the original fan club arranged for a 25th Wedding Anniversary Celebration for Dick and Leigh. The party would be held in a restaurant in suburban Chicago. Dick's mother would also attend the banquet. The evening went off without a hitch — Dick enjoyed the chance of meeting and talking with his old friends and, as always, was thrilled with the new fans that he had attracted. Leigh, though feeling ill, was her usual gracious and charming self.

The following day was Labor Day. While preparing to return to Las Vegas, Leigh became extremely ill. Dick rushed her to an emergency clinic. While the doctors tended to Leigh, Dick called me.

"Bob, Leigh is terribly ill and I've got to take her to a hospital in Chicago. Can you help me out?"

Knowing that Dick would need transportation while Leigh was in the hospital, I called Al Waltner to ask if he had a car that Dick could borrow. Understanding the urgency of the situation, Waltner arranged to provide Dick with a vehicle.

Arriving at the clinic in Schaumburg, I waited with my friend. When Leigh was released, the doctor handed Dick a prescription for medication that would combat her nausea.

The doctor told Dick that he should have it filled immediately. Because of the holiday, most pharmacies were closed and he didn't know where to turn.

Luckily, my wife remembered that Woodfield Mall was near the clinic and suggested that a pharmacy could be found there.

Dick hurried to the shopping center, located a pharmacy, and had the prescription filled. After taking the medication,

Leigh began to feel a little better. Thinking that she might be able to keep down some food, the group stopped at a restaurant in Chicago for a light lunch.

During the luncheon, while Dick had left the table, Leigh leaned over to me.

"You know, Bob," she whispered, "I'm so worried about what's going to happen. I'm not so much afraid for myself, but, I just don't know what'll happen to Dick — he depends so much on me that, if I should die, I don't know how he'd handle things."

I told the wonderful lady that she shouldn't worry about such things. I told her that she needed to concentrate her efforts on getting well.

She looked at me with a winsome smile that I'll never forget, as if she knew that, never again would she be well."

"Okay, Bob," she smiled, patting her friend's arm, "we'll see how things turn out."

The following day, Leigh was admitted to Chicago's Northwestern Memorial Hospital for tests. In a short time, the doctors knew that the cancer had returned. They recommended that Dick take Leigh back home.

Dick arranged for Leigh to be admitted to Cedars-Sinai Hospital in Los Angeles. The physicians there were among the very best in the country and Dick wanted her to have the very best.

Arriving in LA, Dick and Leigh were greeted by the faithful Barbara Stuart. Because she saw no purpose in Dick's returning to Las Vegas, Stuart offered him the use of her guest house while Leigh was hospitalized. Dick gratefully accepted the generous offer.

Although the doctors did everything that they could and Leigh put up a valiant fight, the cancer, spreading like wild-fire, raged through her body and could not be contained.

On May 16, 1982, at two o'clock in the morning, I received a call from Dick. In a tearful voice, the entertainer said that his beloved Leigh had succumbed to the dreaded disease.

"She was the most important thing in my life," Dick whispered, "the mother of my children; the most loving and supportive wife that any man ever had."

"You know, Bob," Dick rambled on, "I remember ... she was so beautiful ... I'd stay awake at night and watch her sleeping. I loved her so and now she's gone!"

Though I wanted to be, I was of little help to my long-time friend in his hour of loss. I, too, was shattered by the news of Leigh's death. Though I tried, I couldn't think of any words to help ease my dear friend's anguish. I had loved Leigh like a sister ... now she was gone.

Sitting hundreds of miles apart, tears streaming down our cheeks, Dick and I sat quietly, each understanding the enormity of the tragic loss.

Although trying to maintain a sense of stability for his family's sake, Dick found it hard to go on without Leigh.

CHAPTER TWENTY-EIGHT
SURPRISE!!!

In November of 1982, a few short months after Leigh's death, Dick returned to California for a series of performances at the L.G.T. (Let's Go To) Vegas supper club in the valley community of Mission Hills. Dick had performed many times at the club and always played to a packed room.

While Dick was performing at L.G.T.'s, I made a trip to southern California to visit my brother who resided there. I arranged to attend one of Dick's performances and was thrilled to see the SRO crowd.

Before the show, Dick walked over to my table and we exchanged small talk the way that good friends do.

"Hey, Dick," I said, "the place is packed! I'm so happy for you."

Dick smiled and nodded. He told me that the crowds had been great and that celebrities had been in attendance at nearly every show.

"By the way," he whispered, "do you know who's sitting at the table right behind you?"

I turned to see a beautiful lady wearing a magnificent red evening gown and fabulous jewelry. She caught my eye and gave me a smile. Embarrassed, I turned to Dick.

"She's a beautiful lady, Dick," I said. "And she looks familiar. I can't place her, though."

Dick leaned closer.

"Bob, that's Gloria DeHaven — the movie actress. I used to

date her when I first came to Hollywood in the early fifties."

"Come on, I'll introduce you to her."

Dick took me by the hand and we turned to Miss DeHaven's table.

"Hi, Gloria," Dick said. "I'm glad you could come to the show this evening."

"I wouldn't miss it, Dick!" the beauty smiled. "The reviews say that your show is a must see."

After exchanging some small talk, Dick introduced me to her.

"This is my friend, Bob," he told her. "He's visiting from Chicago."

The actress took my hand and told me that she was pleased to make my acquaintance.

The lights dimmed and showtime was near. Dick left to go backstage and after saying good-bye to Miss DeHaven, I returned to my table.

Dick performed for nearly an hour and the audience acknowledged each number with wild applause. As he prepared to close the show, Dick thanked the audience for attending the show and extending an invitation to join him for a late breakfast at a nearby restaurant. With that, he began playing the instantly recognizable notes of "The American Trilogy."

At the song's finish, the crowd jumped to its feet. Dick waved his thanks, blew kisses to the audience and disappeared backstage.

"Excuse me, Bob," a voice said.

I turned. It was the beautiful DeHaven standing beside my table. She said that she wanted to ask me two questions.

"Was Dick serious about inviting his fans to join him for breakfast?" she asked.

"Sure," I responded. "He's done that for years. He loves meeting his audience. He feels that it creates a bond between them that translates into the warmth that's felt at every show."

"How marvelous!" she sighed. "Although my date and I have other plans, I wish that we could take Dick up on his offer."

"You had another question?"

"Oh, yes. Is that handsome young man who accompanies Dick on the drums really his son?

I explained that the drummer was, indeed, Dick's son, Peter.

"He's a very handsome young man," the actress exclaimed. "I wonder if he'd like to meet my daughter..."

With that, she offered me her hand and walked away.

••••••••••

The crowds that Dick attracted to the supper club caused the owners of L.G.T.'s to extend Dick's engagement for an indefinite period.

As the days turned into weeks, crowds flocked to see the man who personified dynamic showmanship. Each evening, hundreds of fans came to enjoy Dick's performance. Once again, after thirty years, Dick had risen to become the hottest entertainment ticket in southern California.

Although still broken hearted over the loss of his beloved Leigh, Dick cast aside his personal sorrow as he thrilled audiences the way he had decades before at Ciro's and The Mocambo. Each night, stalwarts of the entertainment industry — people like Rudy Vallee, Piper Laurie, Anthony Caruso, and Paul Picerni — joined Dick's fans in cheering on the maestro.

At the start of the second month of Dick's SRO engagement, the owners of the supper club, Hank and Louise Arklin, joined with many of Dick's friends in the entertainment industry in planning a celebration of Dick's thirty-fifth anniversary in show business. At first, the organizers were unsure as to Dick's enthusiasm for such an event. They knew that some performer's, like some people, didn't enjoy the marking of an anniversary — the passing of time served as a reminder of their mortality. Dick, however, would harbor no such fears.

Hank Arklin gave me a call one afternoon, and asked what I thought of the surprise anniversary celebration. I told him that I thought that it was a great idea and said that Dick would be thrilled with the celebration."

I told Arklin that I was only sorry that I couldn't do anything to be a part of the show. To my surprise, however, Arklin told me that I could play a most important part in the program by providing something that he hadn't been able to find anywhere else.

"Bob, I've heard that you have a taped recording of the finals of the Horace Heidt contest that Dick won in 1948."

"Sure, I've got the tape."

"Listen," the Californian continued, "will you lend it to me to use during the anniversary show? Horace Heidt's going to be there and I know that the tape will provide many pleasant memories for Heidt and for all of the people who'll attend."

I readily agreed to lend Arklin my copy of the cherished tape. My only condition was that the tape be returned immediately after the show.

In the grand scheme of the evening, my tape was just a little thing. I was very happy to have played even a minor role in the celebration of my dear friend's show business anniversary.

SURPRISE!!!

On December 7, 1982, exactly thirty-five years to the day after his first appearance on the Horace Heidt Original Youth Opportunity Program, Dick witnessed another SRO crowd jam into the L.G.T. Vegas showroom to honor him. The entertainer, unaware of the planned festivities, spoke to several people backstage about the unusual number of celebrities at the show and it was all that Arklin could do not to reveal the surprise.

At the appointed time, Dick took the stage to a thunderous round of applause from the enthusiastic audience.

"Everywhere I looked," he says, "there was a familiar face. Frank DeVol, Roberta Sherwood, Pete Condoli, Dick Van Patten, Paul Picerni, Tony Caruso ... I knew that I'd better put on a good show for an audience filled with such heavy hitters."

And that's exactly what he did. For over two hours Dick held the packed room spellbound, playing and singing, entertaining as only he could. As he closed the show with "The American Trilogy," the celebrity-studded audience leapt to its feet in a heartfelt outburst of affection and appreciation. Dick Van Patten, the star of Broadway, motion pictures, and the successful television series, "Eight Is Enough," seemed to speak for the entire room when he said, "What a show ... he's the most incredible entertainer I've ever seen."

Following the ovation, Dick was called back to the stage by famed Character Actor Anthony Caruso, the man who would serve as the evening's Master of Ceremonies.

"Dick," Caruso said, "I'm sure that you realize that this was a special evening. Tonight, your friends and fans have come together to celebrate this, the thirty-fifth anniversary of your start in show business."

Dick, with tears in his eyes, embraced the actor, a move that brought another roar from the capacity crowd.

Next, Caruso introduced many of the celebrities in attendance, although he saved the evening's biggest surprise for last.

"And, finally," Caruso said, "we have a gentleman who's traveled here to be with you on this special night — a man who was instrumental in introducing you to the American people."

It was then that the tape of Dick's victory in the 1948 Grand Finals was played. As the recording ended, Caruso roared into the microphone, "Ladies and gentlemen, here he is — eighty-two years young — Mr. Horace Heidt!"

Dick's surprise was apparent as the ever-dapper Heidt made his way onto the stage. Dick had never lost his affection for the man nor had he failed to afford Heidt his due in creating the "Contino Phenomenon."

Remembering Dick's performances, Heidt praised the entertainer, saying, "if Dick's early performances had been televised — if the nation had had the opportunity of not only hearing, but also seeing this great performer — then, believe me, Dick Contino would have been several years ahead of Elvis Presley in claiming international superstardom."

"I was so happy to see Mr. Heidt," Dick recalls. "When he put his arms around me, it was as if the years had melted away."

The anniversary program continued with tributes from many of the celebrities in attendance, performances by Comedian Jimmy Caesar and Singer Adrienne Leonetti, and, finally, a resolution from the California State Senate honoring Dick for "his outstanding performances and accomplishments in the entertainment field."

"That evening was," Dick says, "one of the treasured moments of my life."

The next few hours became a "love fest" as Dick greeted the many friends and fans who had made the celebration such a never-to-be-forgotten event.

When the evening had ended and Dick finally had the chance to visit with his family, he was emotionally drained by the honor that had been accorded him.

"Sharing such a celebration with my family and friends meant so much to me," Dick remembers. "All that kept it from being a perfect evening was that my beautiful, wonderful wife wasn't there to share it with me."

As he left the club early that morning, Dick's thoughts kept drifting back towards those summer days in Covington, Tennessee — glorious days spent with his beloved Leigh.

CHAPTER TWENTY-NINE
MISSED YOU

In March of 1984, I called Dick to inform him that the Knights of Columbus Council in Oak Lawn, Illinois was interested in having Dick appear as the headliner at its annual fund raising event.

Dick readily agreed to the appearance. A few weeks later, he was on a plane headed for O'Hare Field.

While driving him to the show, I put a leading question to him.

"Dick, what would you think about performing at a festival that I'll be putting on in July?"

The question took Dick by surprise.

"You serious, Bob? Tell me more."

I explained that I had approached Paul Iannelli about the idea of promoting an Italian festival in South Chicago Heights. Iannelli had urged me to pursue the idea and offered to help in any way that he could.

"That sounds great, but you have to remember, Bob, that the Milwaukee Festa is also in July. I hope you're not thinking of competing against them."

I assured my friend that, of course, the festas would be on different dates. If Iannelli was going to help him, then the event couldn't be scheduled for the same weekend as the Milwaukee extravaganza.

It was planned that Dick would headline the entertainment for the South Chicago Heights Festa. Other acts would include The Four Aces, Christine Correlli, and several local performers. The festival would, of course, be a celebration of the Italian culture, featuring traditional foods, crafts, and games and rides for the children.

I spent the intervening months arranging the fest. With Dick as the headliner, interest in the festival ran to a fever pitch. After Dick's triumphant concerts of three years before, people were excited at the opportunity of seeing him again.

Each time I encountered a problem, Iannelli was there to lend a helping hand — securing entertainers; dealing with the logistics of putting on the event; bringing in food vendors, musicians, and sound men; arranging for sponsorship for the festival's entertainment stage — Iannelli was everywhere.

Without Paul's support and encouragement, and without the assistance of my family and friends, the festival would never have gotten off the ground.

With excellent entertainment, great food and perfect weather, the festa drew large and appreciative audiences. Dick had the people eating out of the palm of his hand. After every performance, he walked through the festa grounds, enjoying the adulation that came his way.

For each of the three days of the fest, the event's attendance grew. People came from as far away as Florida and New York to attend the festival. My brother, Shinze, and his wife, Virginia, flew in from California to join in the fun and to visit with family and old friends.

The Four Aces, Correlli and Dick put on marvelous shows and, when the event ended each evening, people hated to go home.

"The Festa was a great time," Dick says. "The warmth of the audiences and the "spirito" of the people made it a very special time for me."

"Of course," Dick adds, "knowing that I was helping out one of my best and dearest friends made the event all the more special."

••••••••••

Due to the success of the 1984 South Chicago Heights Italian Festa, plans were made to repeat the event the following year. Once again, I would coordinate the celebration. My first choice for a headliner for the festa was, of course, Dick Contino.

I called Dick to let him know him about the festa. After telling him about all of the people who were wondering if he would return, I asked if he'd be interested in headlining the entertainment.

To my surprise, Dick hedged.

"Bob," the entertainer said, "I had a great time at your festa and I'd love to do it again, but I've got a little problem."

Dick went on to explain to me that there was a chance that he would be booked for that year's Italian Festa in Chicago and that Anthony Fornelli didn't like to schedule entertainers who had performed in the immediate area in the month preceding the festa.

"I think I'll have to take a rain check this year, Bob."

I told him that I understood his problem and that he needn't be upset about his inability to appear at the event. I went right ahead with plans for the Festa. Stumped as to whom I would get to headline the event, I found my answer while looking through the newspaper.

As I was reading the entertainment section of the Sunday Edition Chicago Tribune, I noticed that Frank Sinatra, Jr. was appearing at a Chicago night club.

"Connie!" I called to my wife, "Here's our headliner."

Connie agreed.

"That'd be great! I'd love to get Frank Sinatra, Jr. to be our headliner."

Jumping into action, I called the club and found out where Sinatra was staying. Contacting the singer, I discussed the Festa with him and asked if he'd be interested in headlining the event.

"Mr. Bove," the young singer said, "I like the idea of appearing at the festival, and think that it would be great to appear at an Italian event."

Sinatra, Jr. told me to contact his Los Angeles-based Agent Vince Carbone, and that, if the dates were free, he'd be willing to appear.

When I contacted Carbone, I explained to the agent that I was interested in booking the singer as headliner for the Festa.

"That's great, Bob," Carbone said, "I'm sure that we can work out something."

The agent told Bob that the singer's fee would be $15,000 for the three days and that Sinatra, Jr. wanted a twenty-piece orchestra, and that first-class hotel accommodations were to be provided.

After a moment of silence, I responded to the demands.

"Vince," I said, "thanks for your time."

I began to hang up the phone when Carbone's voice shot through the line.

"Bob, Bob," the man said, "what's wrong?"

"Listen, Vince, $15,000 is way out of line."

"But, Bob ...."

I cut the agent short.

"Vince, we're a small festival - it's just our second year. We don't have a lot of money. We're more interested in promoting our Italian heritage then we are in promoting Frank

Sinatra, Jr."

The agent was silent for a while.

"I hear you," Carbone said, finally. "Tell me, Bob, what are you willing to offer?"

"$5,000."

"Come on, Bob," the agent said, "I mean, five grand is nothing."

"It's all that I can afford."

Sighing, the agent told me that he would contact Sinatra, Jr. to let him know of the offer. Then he would inform me of the singer's decision.

A few days later, Carbone called me.

"Bob," he said, "great news - you've got Frank Sinatra, Jr. as the headliner for your festa."

"He agreed? For $5,000?"

"Yep."

"Send me the contract — we'll get things going."

••••••••••

As the weeks passed, I continued to work assiduously in organizing the fest. I arranged the event's food, refreshments, and children's entertainment.

In early June, I came home from work to learn that Dick had phoned me. My wife said that Dick had mentioned that he wouldn't be appearing at Chicago's Italian Festa that year.

I was shocked.

"Connie, I'd love to have Dick appear at our Festa but, with the arrangements already made, we just haven't the money."

"God," I added quietly, "I wish I did."

With Sinatra, Jr., the Four Aces, Christine Correlli, the backup musicians, and a new stage that had been rented for the event,

Dick playing accordian

I had already exhausted my entertainment budget and simply could not afford to add my friend to the roster of talent.

A few weeks before the fest was to take place, I received a phone call from one of Dick's fans. The lady, upset that the entertainer would not be appearing at the festival, vented her anger on me.

"Look," I told the woman, "I just can't afford to book Dick Contino with the other acts I've signed. Let's face it, he's one of my dearest friends, I'd love to have him at the Festa."

The lady still was not satisfied.

"What do you mean you don't have the money? I heard that you didn't pay Dick last year ..."

I interrupted her.

"What do you mean, I didn't pay him? Where'd you hear that? I cleared $1,500 last year, donated nearly half of that to the Italian Cultural Center in Stone Park, and paid Dick $4,100. For Christ's sake, he made three times what the other performers made."

"Look lady, I don't know who gave you your information but, whoever it was, they were wrong."

Although upset, I explained that there was still a chance that Dick Contino could play the festa if his fans and members of the Original Fan Club would chip in to cover Dick's appearance fee. The days passed, however, and nobody responded to the suggestion.

So, a few weeks later, with Dick Contino nowhere in sight, the festa took place. In spite of Herculean efforts, the affair was but a shadow of the one that had preceded it.

"We had some bad breaks. The weather that weekend was terrible and, of course, attendance suffered."

Things just didn't work out but, let's face it, that's the chance you take when you promote an outdoor event.

••••••••••

After the festa, things cooled between us. Dick felt that I had let him down. But, I felt that I did the best I could under the circumstances.

Although our friendship had soured, I did make it a point of going to see Dick each time he performed in the Chicago area or at the Milwaukee festa, even though I didn't meet with him personally.

Several years had passed and still our friendship lagged.

One day, while I was attending the festa in Milwaukee, I ran into Fred Diodati, the lead singer of The Four Aces.

"Hey," Diodati told me after the pair had exchanged pleasantries, "I heard that you and Dick are on the outs. Is that so?"

I told the singer that what he'd heard was true.

"I miss him a lot though, Fred. I can't tell you how many times I wanted to call him — but, every time I picked up the phone, I just couldn't do it."

Diodati smiled sympathetically.

"Bob, listen to what I'm telling you. Life's too short to waste a good friendship. If you get the chance, talk with Dick. Believe me, he'd like that."

Thinking over Diodati's words, I wasn't sure what to do. All that day, walking the festival grounds, I kept hearing the singer's words. Several times I started for the stage where Dick was scheduled to perform but, each time I was about to go in, I shook my head and walked away.

Then, the very next day, Corky Bennett, Dick's keyboardist, ran into me at the festa. He, too, told me that I should stop by to see Dick.

"Believe me, Bob," Bennett said, "Dick would really like to see you. He talks about you all of the time."

After his conversation with Bennett, I was torn, wondering what to do.

I walked around the whole afternoon, trying to figure out when I should see Dick, *if* I should see Dick, and what I'd say when I saw him.

Finally, I strolled to the Pabst Stage for Dick's four o'clock performance. I was still unsure of how to proceed.

I wanted to get together with Dick, but I wasn't sure that

Dick and Bob Bove

he felt the same way. After all, he hadn't made any effort to contact me! Suppose he didn't want to see me again?

It was one of the most trying hours of my life.

I decided to watch as Dick worked his magic, treating his fans to a rousing show. An hour later, as Dick finished his performance, I was swept up by the throng of fans rushing towards the stage to secure the entertainer's autograph.

Head bowed, Dick signed his name again and again. I blended into the throng of autograph seekers. Somewhat tentatively, I thrust out my hand.

"Mr. Contino," I said softly, "I don't have any paper — would you sign my hand?"

Surprised by the request, Dick looked up to see his old friend's smiling face. At that instant, the years of discord were stripped away. Dick jumped to his feet and hugged me, telling me of how happy he was to see me.

"Stay here, Bob!" Dick said when the autograph session was finished, "Stay right here! We'll go grab something to eat. We've got lots to catch up on."

Like the stain that disappears in the laundry, the animosity between the men had disappeared and all that remained was a clean, beautiful feeling.

EPILOGUE

And now, nearly a half century after bursting onto the entertainment scene, Dick Contino continues to perform — drawing large, enthusiastic and appreciative audiences wherever he appears.

As this book is being finished, Dick has been performing with Al Martino and The Gaylords at Florida venues in Fort Myers, Daytona Beach and Boca Raton. He is booked for future appearances at the Palace Station in Las Vegas.

This year, fans are looking forward to his appearances at Milwaukee's Italian festa (where he's revered as Mr. Festa); at ethnic celebrations in major cities and in smaller towns throughout the country; and at nightclubs in Las Vegas, and Atlantic City.

Once, I asked Dick if he'd ever thought about retiring from show business. I'll never forget how he answered me.

"Bobby," he replied, "as long as God gives me the ability to perform, and as long as the people keep coming to see me, I'll never retire. They'll have to carry me off the stage!"

"Like my Dad told me just before he passed away in September of 1973, if you take care of your mind and body, if you let time work for you and not against you, then, like wine, you become better with age. If you don't, you become like vinegar."

"I've always done my best to follow that advice and I feel that, like fine wine, my music and I get better with age."

So, if ever you should decide to attend one of Dick's performances — be sure to tell him that Bob Bove sent you.

Dick Contino

Credits and Accomplishments

* Grand Prize Winner -

  Horace Heidt Youth Opportunity Program Finals -
  December 7, 1948

* Performed in every major showroom in America

* Performance at The Hollywood Bowl

* Star of Ed Sullivan's tour of the Soviet Union

* Films:

  "Daddy-O"
  "Girl's Town"
  "Big Night"

* Television (Drama):

  "Night Song" - Lux Video Theater - NBC
  Days of Our Lives

* Television (Variety)

  The Ed Sullivan Show (a record 48 appearances)
  The Hollywood Palace
  The Merv Griffin Show
  The Joey Bishop Show
  The Art Linkletter Show

* Nightclubs:

  The Flamingo Hotel - Las Vegas
  The Tropicana Hotel - Las Vegas
  The Sahara Hotel - Las Vegas
  The Frontier Hotel - Las Vegas
  Harrah's - Reno
  Harrah's - Lake Tahoe
  Harrah's - Atlantic City

* Two tours to Vietnam to entertain troops

* Appearance at Dodger Stadium
  (Our National Anthem)

* Sixteen-month tour of duty in Korea

* Twenty albums on major labels:

Presenting Dick Contino and His Accordion

Sabre Dance
El Relicario
Peggy O'Neill
Tea for Two
Roman Guitar
Beer Barrel Polka

Accordion Magic

I Wonder, I Wonder
I'm Beginning to See the Light
Cool Water
Sentimental Me
Til I Waltz Again With You
She's Funny That Way
I Almost Lost My Mind
Fascination
Dark Eyes
Flight of the Bumble Bee
Blues In F
Hava Nagila

Plays & Sings The Hits

I Know A Place
King of the Road
People
The Girl From Ipanema
A Hard Day's Night
Dear Heart
Red Roses For A Blue Lady
Downtown
My Favorite Things
Pizza Pie
My Baby
Night Train

Dick Contino at the Fabulous Flamingo/Las Vegas

Lady of Spain
Ebb Tide
Swingin' on a Star
Come Back to Sorrento
Peg O' My Heart
Peggy O'Neil
Flying Home
Ciribiribin
Begin the Beguine
Baby, Baby, All The Time
Nature Boy
Arrivederci, Roma

South American Holiday
w/ David Carroll & Orchestra

Sweet and Gentle
Brazil
Come Closer To Me
Delicato
Brazilian Polka
A Media Luz
Adios Mu Cha Cha
Tico Tico
Ay, Ay, Ay
Mama Eu Quero
Caminito
Down Argentina Way

Polka Time

Clarinet Polka
Liechtensteiner Polka
Let Me Call You Sweetheart
Hand Clap Polka
Woodpecker Song
Just Because
Beer Barrel Polka
Helena Polka
Flight of the Angels
Pennsylvania Polka
Blue Skirt Waltz
Hot Pretzels

Hawaiian Holiday

Love Song from "Mutiny on the Bounty"
Sweet Leilani
Hawaiian War Chant
Farewell For Just A While
Diamond Head
Blue Hawaii
The Hukilau Song
The Hawaiian Wedding Song
My Little Grass Shack
Tropical Quiet Village
Aloha Oe

ACCORDION MAN

Roman Holiday

Volare
Santa Lucia
I Have But One Heart
Cielito Song
Innamorata
Arrivederci Roma
Non Dimenticar
O Sole Mio
Bella Melodia
Return To Me
Neapolitan Nights
Ciribiribin

An Accordion In Paris

Two Loves Have I
Mam'Selle
The Petite Waltz
Comme Ci Comme Ca
My Man
The Song from "Moulin Rouge"
Beyond The Sea
Under The Bridges of Paris
Blues from "An American In Paris"
Symphony
Domino
Parlez Moi D'Amour

Something For The Girls
w/ David Carroll

Twilight Time
Mexicali Rose
Nightingale
Song of the Islands
Tango of the Roses
Bewitched
Poinciana
The One Finger Melody
You Are Always In My Heart
Purple Islands
Adios
Charmaine

It's Dance Time

The Object of My Affection
Cachita
Sunrise Serenade
Linger Awhile
Amapola
Say It With Music
By The Light of the Silvery Moon
Rain on the Roof
Moonlight Cocktail
Brazil
Nola
Moonlight and Roses

Twelve Immortal Songs

Moon River
To Each His Own
Yours
Stardust
Moonglow
Deep Purple
Sentimental Journey
Blue Tango
Ruby
Tenderly
Canadian Sunset
Begin the Beguine

Dick Contino / Horace Heidt

Malaguena
Jalousie
Caravan
Tarantella
Toselli's Serenade
Lover
12th Street Rag
Clarinet Polka

Dick Contino / Horace Heidt

Contino Boogie
Twilight Time
Lady of Spain
Sorrento
Czardas
Canadian Capers
Sunrise Serenade
Ciribiribin

Twilight Time

Sleepy Time Gal
Tumbling Tumbleweeds
Chapel By The Sea
Stranger on the Shore
Twilight Time
Dream
Sweet Georgia Brown
My Happiness
Oh What It Seemed To Be
Rumors Are Flying
Sunrise Serenade
Peg O' My Heart

ACCORDION MAN

On Stage

Hey Look Me Over
76 Trombones
Mala Femmena
The Bells of St. Mary's
Old Man Time
Exodus
Paree
More
Never On Sunday
Mama
Granada

Squeeze Me

Yesterdays
Bring Back The Thrill
Theme From Lombardo Ending
Pagan Love Song
Gone With The Wind
Whispering
Dream
My Melancholy Baby
In The Shade of the Old Apple Tree
Little White Lies
I Wonder I Wonder I Wonder
Blue Moon

Italia

La Novia
La Spagnola
Quando Quando Quando
La Paloma
Tico Te Tico Ta
Reginella Campagnola
Cara Mia
Torna A Sorriento
La Chitarra Romana
Oh! Ma Ma (with Papa Contino)
Se Piangi, Si Ridi (with Leigh Snowden)
Al Di La

In The Mood

Woodchopper's Ball
Blues In The Night
In The Mood
Miserlou
Johnson Rag
Sentimental Journey
Peridio
Mood Indigo
Jersey Bounce
Cherokee
Come Back To Sorrento
String of Pearls

ACCORDION MAN

Yours

Yours
New York, New York
My Kingdom
Beer Barrel Polka
She Believes In Me
Lady of Spain
Twilight Time
What It Is
Contino Boogie
Help Yourself
Battle Hymn of the Republic/Dixie